GERMANY
AFTER HITLER

BY
PAUL HAGEN

FARRAR & RINEHART, INC.
NEW YORK   TORONTO

To Anna

Contents

GERMANY
AFTER HITLER

I. The Case of a Retarded Democracy:

BLACK records as well as white records of entire nations, as they are usually turned out in wartime, give but little enlightenment. At best they are sentimental clichés, pretending to be historical truths. They interpret history emotionally. There is little in them on which to base political strategy or on which to achieve future security.

Are there two Germanies? The black record denies it emphatically. The white record, on the other hand, is obviously guilty of presenting too pious a picture. We shall find a hard-boiled answer only by restudying the history of Germany's retarded and interrupted democratization. Few people realize that Germany's problem has always been the problem of a country situated not only geographically, but also politically, between the West and the East, between the more modern and the more archaic world. For centuries she lagged behind the nations of the West. After a fresh start at the close of the last war she suffered the Hitler setback. In the meanwhile even Russia had advanced. The present Germany has thus quite naturally developed an affinity to Japan, a country in which modern and archaic societies find a classic form of co-existence.

If we examine history we discover that a basic conflict has existed in Germany for a long time. The archaic Germany, which was beaten in 1918 and restored to streamlined design under Hitler, has never ceased to exist. Germany's quick, superficial modernization in the second half of the nineteenth century did not wipe it out, and the postwar period did not wipe it out. In this respect Germany shows a marked similarity to Japan where the most modern economic and technical development was grafted on to the ancient society of the Samurai. Of course, the cases are not identical. Germany even now stands somewhere between the nations of the western world and Japan. In common with other western nations, her old feudal institutions underwent a degree of democratization before her industrial revolution. Germany's industrialization started later than England's, but once it started it went on at a breath-taking pace. Its speed had the effect of accentuating her inner conflicts, not liquidating them. Even more stormy was Japan's industrialization. Beginning still later than Germany, she thrust herself out of her medieval calm into an aggressive program of modern industrial imperialism. Technically modernized, her roots remained unbroken in her feudal past. The feudal past of Germany has been shaken. But her privileged castes and cliques, like the Samurai in Japan, have survived and reached out into the new world as a relic of ancient absolutism.

This is the background of the existence of two Germanies.

In modern times, the conflict between the two Germanies has gone on unremittingly. One Germany had roots deep in the democratic movements and in the growing drive for emancipation from absolutism that stirred the western world. The other Germany was the unbroken archaic Germany of predemocratic absolutism. During the modern industrial period, the leadership of the first Germany passed to the labor movement, the strongest in Europe at that time. However, like the German liberals of earlier periods, German labor challenged but never broke the power of the feudal castes and cliques which, in fact, gained strength by the addition to their ranks of the new industrial barons. The inner conflict continued until the defeat of Germany in the last war. Then, for the first time in modern history, aggressive imperialist Germany, led by the surviving medieval German Samurais seemed to be broken. Unfortunately, it was in appearance only. The social and economic position of Germany's privileged castes was only touched by the revolution of 1918. They abdicated politically for a time. After their restoration they helped Hitler into power.

The present Germany has often been compared to France of 1800, Hitler to Napoleon, and Nazism to Bonapartism. There is, indeed, a fascinating parallel between France at the beginning of the nineteenth century and Germany today which calls for an explanation. In both cases, we have societies in transition from feudal absolutism to democracy, both went through previous revolts against absolutism. In both cases, early immature democratic forces were overrun by counterrevolutions. In both cases, the counterrevolution was not simply reactionary but the bastard of revolutionary and reactionary forces. In both cases, the chief aim was nationalistic expansion. The youth of France of 1800 was fascinated by the messiah Napoleon as the German youth of 1933 was fascinated by the messiah Hitler. The glory of Napoleon's early victories seduced the French people no less than the glory of Hitler seduced the German people during the period of the Nazi blitz victories. Napoleon became First Consul in 1799 and submitted his newly fabricated "Constitution" to the verdict of the people. He received an affirmative vote of 3,011,017 against the votes of only 1,567 Frenchmen who openly opposed him. This is strongly reminiscent of the 99 per cent Hitler vote of a few years ago. Both Napoleon's and Hitler's forces were cruel and ruthless. The reputation of Napoleon after the lapse of more than a century is not as bad as Hitler's today. But to contemporary Germans, Russians and English, he was the "tyrant, the anti-Christ, the murderer, the liar, the public nuisance, the enemy of mankind." Napoleon's guards went through an early training in a period of white terror, the terror following the overthrow of the Jacobins. The Hitler guards received their training in a period of white terror, the *Fehme* murders following the mild revolution of 1918 in Germany. The pattern of aggressive nationalism in each case was built upon the same foundations. Even the symbols—the eagles and the mass production of field marshals— are identical. And similar, too, is the legacy of hatred left in the hearts of the victim nations.

These similarities in appearance could not exist without a more fundamental parallel. The twentieth century, of course, is very different from the early nineteenth century. There is little in common between the late capitalism of contemporary Europe and the early capitalism of the France of one hundred and fifty years ago. Different groups and classes played historic roles in the two periods. The relative strength of the European powers is different, and so too is the national character of the French and the German people. And the two wars are different—the one provoked by the forces of Napoleon and the other by the forces of Hitler —different in dimensions, in character and in consequences. But the parallel which exists is too obvious to overlook. We shall understand its basic characteristics after a more concrete analysis of the history of Germany. We shall see that history as a classic example of delayed and retarded democratization, so that Germany today is a country much closer to Japan than to its western European neighbors, and therefore really again, as under the Kaiser, in a Bonapartist phase.

It is true that her economic system, her industrial technique, her social organization is western, but so is that of Japan. Germany is the most highly developed country in the Axis coalition. Her scientists are able to smash atoms and to produce synthetically many of the commodities which nature did not place in her soil. Her technicians are excellent. Her industrial organization before the war could only be compared with the most modern American organization. There is a modern industrial proletariat, with a political history of a seventy-year struggle for emancipation. Its organizations have been smashed, and its leadership beaten and broken. Even under Hitler, with German labor robbed of its privileges, Germany has conserved a good part of her social reforms and a modern system of social security, developed during seven decades of rapid industrialization and technical modernization. But like Japan she had never fully liquidated the vestiges of feudal absolutism.

The first democratic republic in Germany failed under the attack of the alliance of her medieval landed aristocracy, her great industrialists and the military cliques. The same combination of forces supplied the motive power for the aggression of the Kaiser Reich. Only recently it has been pointed out how surprisingly "Hitlerite" the early imperialistic period of Germany was. Pan-Germanistic documents that were published during the nineties have been found to contain in nucleus almost everything which we have come to know as Nazi doctrine. The Pan-Germanist school was not identical with the reactionary coalition ruling the Kaiser's Reich but it supplied the ideologists of German imperialism. In their books you find anti-Semitism, antiliberalism, antiunionism. These men are not the ideologists of a capitalist and bourgeois age. They are the spiritual relics of feudal philosophy. You find them sprinkled through democratic countries too—all have their Ku Klux Klans, their Christian Frontists, their Huey Longs, their racial discrimination. Hardheaded monopolists and colonial imperialists everywhere are fond of the same ideas as the reactionaries of Germany. But in the democratic world the outmoded ideas are balanced and over-balanced by democratic institutions and the established traditions of a modern society.

In the Axis world and especially in Germany the ancient society survived the spring storms of the democratic revolutions and the reforms of the last two hundred years. It created a modern power machine and fastened it onto the surviving base of feudal absolutism. In this respect Germany resembles Japan more than it does the West.

The reasons for the delay in the development of German democracy will be clearer when we compare the German process with the developments in the West. The process of democratization in western nations was based on the achievement of national unity, the establishment of civil liberties

and popular democratic rights, and the liquidation of feudal privileges, special prerogatives and
castes. All of these achievements came in Germany
one hundred, sometimes two hundred years, later
than in the western world. The conflicts of Cromwell's time plus Napoleonism plus modern aggressive imperialism characterize the Hitler period.

National unity was achieved in Great Britain
around 1700. The first parliament of united Great
Britain was elected in 1707. That was long before
the industrial age. National unity was achieved
in France under the Bourbon kings. It was completed during the Napoleonic period around
1800. The thirteen colonies in the New World declared their independence and thereby made the
first step toward national unification even earlier.
The first step toward national unity was achieved
in Germany, and only partially then, through
the *Zollverein* in 1832, a second through the
Prussian sword under Bismarck in 1866. Even in
the last war, Bavarian, Saxon and Prussian armies
maintained a separate military organization. The
National Assembly of the Weimar Republic was
unable to overcome the separation of the ancient
states expressed in the *Laender*. In fact, it was
Hitler who completed national unification, but
only as a means towards forging a weapon for
world conquest. At the time of the American
Declaration of Independence Germany was far
from being a nation. She was more like India
today, a territory of 350 odd principalities ruled

by dwarf despots. The shadow of the medieval Holy Roman Emperor sat on his throne in Vienna, presiding over a predominantly non-German empire. His rival was the King of Prussia, then a puppet of one or another of the great powers, France, England, and Russia. Possessed of great ambitions, he inflicted a costly militarism on a poor and small country.

In the western world, democratization was generally achieved before the industrial age. The British parliaments fought persistently through many centuries against British autocracy until finally, with the passage of the habeas corpus acts and the Declaration of Rights in the late seventeenth century, British democracy was firmly established. The decisive factor in democracy's victory was the emancipation of the middle classes. Since then in England democracy has had its ups and downs. And democracy is never perfect and never completely safe. New dangers and threats come up in nearly every new crisis and with every new and important social change. But it is a characteristic of established democracy that it is able to adjust itself in every new crisis and that has been the case in Britain for nearly three centuries. If Britain should go socialist it would remain democratic.

The French development came at least a hundred years later than the English. The last absolutist period in France was between 1600 and 1789 ending in the French Revolution. Since then there have been temporary setbacks—Napoleon, the restoration of the Bourbons, the second Napoleon, Boulanger, the reaction during the Dreyfus affair, and today, in Hitler's shadow, Laval. But these are temporary recessions. French democracy is a living reality, as has been attested for a century and a half and is attested today by the existence of the Free French Committee and the well-organized French underground in France itself.

The first short German democracy came in 1918. Some democratic developments had occurred, of course, in the nineteenth century. There were reforms in 1812 during the fight for liberation against Napoleon. There were reforms during the latter part of the nineteenth century. And for fourteen short years, the first German Republic of Weimar was the freest but also the weakest of all the democratic states. Meanwhile, the enemy waited in ambush. German democracy came into existence only after the defeat of 1918 and was imposed from the outside rather than developed from within. It remained immature and weak. Fourteen years after its inception the revived reactionaries joined forces with Hitler and overthrew it.

In sentimental expositions of the two Germanies, the liberalism of the constitutional monarchy before the last war is very often held up for admiration. Surely, compared with Hitler's tyranny, the Kaiser's Germany appears to old-timers like the golden age of freedom. Even absolutists were not mass murderers like the Nazis. But the constitutional rights of this Germany were very limited rights until 1918. It was a period of a kind of poll-tax franchise, the so-called "three-class suffrage." It was a period of one-party rule, semiliberal in appearance only. When the Allies covered Germany with democratic propaganda during the last war and the home front in Germany began to grumble, the government discussed certain reforms to combat the danger of revolution. In March 1917, to give one example, the Kaiser's government took a daring step. It decided to take *two* "outsiders" into the highest administrative body of the government. One of the two candidates was the Catholic mayor of a large city. He was described in the protocol of the Cabinet meeting as "not too strong a character" and, therefore, the hard-boiled conservatives had no doubt that he would follow their line. This man and a quasi liberal were the only "progressives" to be added to a body of about fifty conservatives. A mighty gulf separated the leaders of the Kaiser Reich from the people just a short time before it fell.

The position of the privileged feudal classes in Germany requires special study. Feudal privileged groups have survived here and there in western democracies. New privileged groups have grown up in the monopolistic era. But their old privileges and their new monopolies have been curtailed by democratic institutions. Where they rule, they cannot rule autocratically. Consider the prerogatives of army officers, as a case in point. In western countries, they are a functional group in the army and are the servants of the country. In Germany, the officers are a privileged feudal caste and have run the country since Prussian militarism emerged about 1700, with a few short interruptions usually following a military defeat. (As a matter of fact, German armies have been defeated more often than their reputation would lead you to believe. They have won many battles and very few wars!) During the last war it was recognized what the German Junker class meant for Germany as the bulwark of its autocracy, not only as an economic force but as master of its military business and the running of the state. These people, "Germany firsters" all, often possessing less than average intelligence, supplied all the leading bureaucrats and most of the officers for the army. They adhered strictly to patriarchic principles. The democratic struggle of their time was only a "fabricated chaos" according to the Crown Prince. The millions of democratic Germans—the majority of the nation—were, in the words of the Kaiser, "enemies of the state." The Hohenzollern family was the first among the Junker families, and in their thinking all the Junkers emulated the first family. Not even the class of the new industrialists, into which the Junkers frequently married for convenience, not even the greatest of the iron and coal barons, were of the same rank. The industrialists, for example, were practically without influence in the foreign policy of the Kaiser Reich and not of too great influence in domestic affairs. This has been forgotten.

It has also been forgotten that after the revolt of 1918 the position of the Junkers only temporarily gave way to social modernization. Germany remained the only country without agrarian reforms. There were agrarian revolutions in Russia, reforms in Lithuania, in Latvia, Rumania and Czechoslovakia, but not in Germany. Soon the Junkers again became the power behind the state and not only in agricultural questions. There were active farmers' movements, but the Junkers overcame them, just as the Junkers in the seventies had gotten the upper hand over the early liberal farmers' movements. The new agrarian organizations remained entirely in the hands of the big landowners. Their high tariff policy, their plundering of state subsidies for their own enrichment, their support of the Free Corps and the Reich murder gangs and later their influence in forming the Hartzburg Front, which was the first open alliance of the Nazi movement and the reactionary forces, dug the grave of the Weimar democracy . They had ruled Germany before 1918. After 1918 they adbicated temporarily to democratic forces but very soon they re-formed the old alliance with the industrial monopolists and obstructed from behind the new throne. Their support for the secret rearmament strangled the democratic reconstruction. And under Hitler, though he curtailed their power, they are still very much alive.

Here you have the parallel with the Japanese Samurai. Germany has never gotten rid of her ancient autocrats. Penetrate the iridescent surface of the fascist party regimes to the bottom and you will find the relics of the predemocratic, even the prebourgeois society of the feudal autocrats. Here are the landed aristocracies, still living off the fat of the land and still driving their countries into aggressive wars if their interests demand it, the Prussian Junkers, the Italian counts, the Japanese knights, the officer castes and bureaucracies. It is their policy and their philosophy. Big business is the other pillar of this alliance. In the early reconstruction period in Germany after the last war, the great industrialists controlled several cabinets. But even at the height of their influence, at the height of the power of finance and industrial capitalism they were never as powerful as the feudal castes. There are people who explain the Hitler war pre-eminently in terms of modern economic imperialism, but this is an oversimplification. The story of how Hitler became Chancellor is too well known. His handmaidens were Junkers, industrialists, bureaucrats and generals. The decisive push came from the Hindenburg clique. It was a Junker intrigue!

The conclusion is this: In western Europe national unification, democratization and the removal of at least the privileges of the feudal autocrats took place several centuries ago. In Germany, on the other hand, the only trend towards centralization developed out of the states with the tradition of military colonies, i.e., in the southeast and in the northeast, out of Austria and Prussia. The national unification was not only delayed but it was effected by traditionally aggressive and reactionary forces; it came in the armor of ancient militarism. Hitler is only the last link in this chain. Hitler rode the wave of a lower-middle-class revolt. This revolt was nationalist because of the defeat, counterrevolutionary because of the resentment against labor's influence in the new state; it was welcomed by the reactionary, revived imperialist bloc. The way toward a new aggression was free.

The weakness of German democratic movements, and their inability to win and to protect a revolution has often been the subject of ridicule. There is very little faith in the coming German revolution now. But this view is based on superficial judgments. True, democratic movements in Germany have come late and they have never yet won the war against German reaction. But they have been strong in the past, they have won many battles and there is no doubt that they will return stronger than ever, and finally win the war. Their delay has been a part of the retarded German development. That was the case with the earliest democratic movements. The Peasant War in England, the Jacquerie in France, came earlier and were more successful than the first German peasant revolt. The English Reformation in the fifteenth century came a hundred years before the German. Until then it may simply have been that Germany's geographical position was the chief delaying factor. The German people, sandwiched in the center of Europe, supplied the battleground for invaders from the East and from the West: they themselves did little invading. In the early centuries they "Christianized," it is true, and were crusaders for the Pope in Rome. They pushed Slavonic tribes back and conquered East Elbian lands. Sometimes they were pushed back. But in later centuries it was different. The Thirty Years' War following the Reformation reduced Germany to a shambles when it ended in 1648. That was when Cromwell's England, a protected island, was developing into a modern nation. France, the profiteer of the Thirty Years' War, developed the grandeur of a big power, the France of Richelieu and the Roi Soleil. It took Germany nearly two hundred years to recover. Her population had fallen from nineteen to five millions. Some regions of Germany had been looted a dozen times. Some of her people lived from human carcasses. The time when she was slowly recovering was the time of the discovery of the sea routes to the West and the development of the transoceanic empires of the western powers.

A new setback occurred during the Napoleonic invasion. It occurred during the period in Germany in which strong spiritual forces had arisen, the great classical period of poets, musicians and philosophers, of Goethe, Lessing, Schiller, Humboldt, and Beethoven. The intellectual leaders of the Germany of that time were blamed too for their inability to get control of political power, but their political weakness derived from Germany's delayed development. Germany was split into three hundred and fifty dwarf tyrannies with which no democratic movement could cope. The first democratic reforms came in the fight against Napoleon, but the war of national liberation itself tended to change hitherto humanistic philosophy into national romanticism. Then came the reactionary period of the Holy Alliance of 1815. Its chief victim was again a German democratic revolution, which finally struggled to the surface in 1848. Alarmed by the liberal activities in Germany, Prince Metternich, the Austrian Minister and the leading statesman of the Congress Europe, in 1819 won over the King of Prussia to the repressive measures known as the Carlsbad Decrees. The decrees bound the individual German sovereigns—who were now reduced in number, but still thirty-six—to control the universities through strict commissioners, to introduce censorship of all publications and to establish a secret inquisition. These decrees postponed constitutional liberty in Germany for a generation. New

movements came in the thirties. At the famous
Hambach Festival, 25,000 Liberals came together,
drank to Lafayette, demanded a republic of German unity and resolved to fight for freedom. Metternich's answer was the adoption of six articles,
imposing on every German sovereign the duty to
reject liberal petitions for constitutional changes.
All public meetings were repressed. Surveillance
of suspicious political characters, called demagogues, was introduced, the edicts against the universities were renewed. Nevertheless, in 1848,
when the whole of Europe was in revolt, revolution swept across the German plains, too. Much
German blood was spilled for freedom. The Revolution was crushed by the Prussian king and the
Prussian army, but not before they had been encouraged by the Czar in Russia and helped by the
Austrian Emperor.

Some liberal developments took place. At the
time of the Gettysburg Address, for instance, Bismarck had to dissolve the Northern German Diet
because this weak democratic body dared to refuse
$12,000,000 which Bismarck asked for the prep-
aration for the Danish War. Then came the German unification through the Prussian sword. The
middle classes, the burghers, were crushed and
liberalism with them. It has never returned since.
But a new, even stronger democratic movement
appeared on the scene, the modern German labor
movement. As a political party it dates back to
1864. After that it became the front-line fighter

against German imperialism, and for a German social democracy. In 1871, August Bebel, its famous leader, went to prison in protest against the annexation of Alsace Lorraine. From 1878 to about 1890 the new movement was outlawed by the Bismarck government, because of its democratic character and its strength. But it survived Bismarck and before the outbreak of World War I it became the strongest democratic party in Germany, with the greatest number of voters in the country. It is well known what happened to it during the last war. It is true it could not prevent the war by a revolution, but no labor party of 1914 could. Not even the Bolsheviks. Some of its leaders broke down politically under the moral pressure of nationalistic enthusiasm in 1914. But other leaders kept the flag high, they went to prison. During the war many of the members of the party resisted the hooray patriotism. By January 1918, the German munitions workers went on strike. It was soldiers, sailors and workers who carried out the revolt of 1918. It is well known that the labor movement stood for all that was progressive in the Weimar Republic.

Labor supplied the largest contingent of the heroic underground in Hitler's Reich and in Hitler's war. They have supplied most of the martyrs —more than the religious groups. Only recently young students and intellectuals have joined them. There cannot be the slightest doubt that after Hitler's defeat the democratic forces will enter a period of reorganization, that they will become the dominant force in German society, if they are permitted by the victors this time to complete the interrupted revolution. Their leading force will be the reborn labor movement.

Why don't they revolt now? Why have even workers and ordinary soldiers committed the most hideous crimes in Hitler's armies? The answer is, they are coerced soldiers and workers and they cannot yet revolt. Why don't the twelve million foreign workers in Germany revolt? More of them are now in German factories than German workers; they certainly cannot be suspected of having Nazi sympathies. It took a long time for foreign contingents of soldiers in German armies to revolt; and there have been whole armies of the vassal nations, like the Rumanians, with Hitler's troops. There is no chance of revolt, as long as to risk revolt means certain death to every participant. The prerequisites for a people's revolt against any tyranny is knowledge that the defeat of the tyrant is near. Fascism, streamlined against democratic forces, is even better organized to keep opposition down, to wipe resistance out if necessary by mass extermination and by the mass executioner, than earlier forms of tyranny and reaction. The periods during which nations under despotic rulers have carried out aggressions, have at the same time been periods of silent martyrdom. There has always been a heroic minority. It has been impotent until the tyrants were about to

fall. Every tyranny contains only the seeds of revolt so long as it is strong. But every tyranny also
is pregnant with a revolution as the end ap-
proaches. Only a short time will pass and this
revolt will come into the open in Germany.

How it will start we know from the Italian experience. No matter how weak it is at the beginning or how exhausted, it will rapidly grow in
strength, unless the victors themselves try to crush
it. The antifascist revolution is like a Caesarean
birth. The surgeon's knife, the intervening army,
is needed to help a child into life. There can be no
revolt without a crushing military defeat of the
Nazi tyranny, but the defeat alone may simply
have an abortive effect; it does not necessarily mean
the rebirth of democratic forces. What is needed
is the cooperation of military victory from outside
and democratic forces from inside. The one is the
job of the United Nations' armies, the other remains the job of the vanquished people themselves. Democratic forces by their own nature
grow only on their own authority. They can't be
imported or delegated, or imposed from one nation to another, even in an interdependent world.
They can, however, be destroyed from outside as
well as by the tyranny within, the common enemy.

We are at a turning point of history. A German
revolt against Hitler is imminent. It will be a part
of the European revolt against Hitler's tyranny
over all Europe. This book describes the major
reasons for its delay. It describes the forces that

will keep it within limits and again create obstacles to its success. Let me repeat, they do not all lie on the German side. And let us hope that this time there shall be more understanding of the importance of a successful democratic revolution than there was in the past. As to mistakes of the past, I offer two examples. The first example is what happened in 1918. From the point of view of the German Nazis and the reactionaries, Allied intervention in 1918 was hated because it initiated the most important step yet to Germany's democratization. They invented the slogan of hate: *November Verbrecher*, criminals of the November revolution. From our point of view another criticism of that period seems more adequate. It is true that the Allied victory established a democracy of the western pattern in Germany. The great majority of the German people then believed in democracy and in Wilson's Fourteen Points. There were posters in the railway stations of little towns such as Halberstadt which greeted returning German troops with the words: *"Seid willkommen tapfre Streiter, Gott und Wilson helfen weiter."* ("Welcome fighters, brave and strong, God and Wilson help along.") And among the people in the Allied countries, there was the earnest desire to make the world safe for democracy.

But not only is democracy generally not an export commodity, the democratization fostered by the Allied command—by the AMG of 1918—

was intentionally a "moderate" democracy. Fear prevailed that Germany would go Bolshevist like Russia. The Allied command wanted to restore law and order in Germany. In occupied territory it banned those political movements likely to endanger the law-and-order regime it preferred —the *Kaiserstaat* minus the Kaiser. It threatened to continue the blockade in case of "Bolshevism." In point of fact, there was no immediate Bolshevist danger in Germany, the best proof of which is the composition of the Congress of Soldiers' and Workers' Councils which met in Berlin in December 1918. The Congress had an overwhelming majority of right-wing Social Democrats, only a small fraction of the more radical and more pacifist left-wing Social Democrats, the Independent Socialists; not a single leader of the German Communists, of the so-called Spartakus League, had been elected. Several months later, during the elections for the National Assembly, the Communists got only one per cent of the votes; in no time during the following hectic fourteen years did they get more than twelve per cent of all the German votes. Right-wing representatives of the Soldiers' and Workers' Councils, rightly or wrongly, pointed out to the Congress that the Entente leaders would refuse to recognize the German "soviets" and thus the conservatives won out.

It is definitely a fact that the compromised representatives of the Kaiser Reich and of the old bourgeois society, including their most reactionary

leaders, were the forces which the Allied representatives wanted to deal with and dealt with. A
contemporary witness of events in the city of
Aachen gave the following account. Aachen (Aix
la Chapelle) is a border town and was the first
place to be occupied. As in all larger cities, a
Workers' and Soldiers' Council had been set up.
It occupied the City Hall and the Administration
buildings. The staff of the French occupation
army appeared at the City Hall and found the
Council in session. Speaking through an interpreter the commanding French general asked the
Council about its credentials. When the men answered that they were the Soldiers' and Workers'
Council and wanted to learn the conditions of the
occupation, the general's face turned purple. He
issued a few commands and the Council members
heard this order: "You have exactly thirty minutes
within which time every old official must be back
in service. You will disband as a Council. If you
have not accomplished this, you will be shot. If
there should be disorder or strikes you will be
held responsible and shot." That was how the
Kaiser's officials were restored in Aachen. Many
German war profiteers, big and small, streamed
from unoccupied territory into the occupied territory. There they felt safe from the German revolution. Among the supernationalists arriving at
the Paris Hotel in Aachen during the first days,
was the famous steel and munitions baron, Kardorf. He registered at this hotel, the headquarters

of the French General Staff, and they lived peacefully together under one roof. (This Kardorf, by the way, became one of Hitler's first supporters, helping him financially long before Thyssen and Krupp. He still is one of the leaders of Hitler's economic staff today.) There were lesser lights, many of the enthusiastic nationalists of the Kaiser party, the chauvinists of Ludendorff's war, who came and entertained the French officers.

At the same time, in Aachen, the occupation troops went right to the headquarters of the trade unions. They did not leave a door or a piece of furniture whole. Trade-union officials and members who happened to be in the offices at the time were lined up, faces against the wall. There they stood for two hours until, the search finished, they were taken to Rheindalen, the local prison camp. There they were kept for five months and the treatment suffered there led one to hang himself and two others to cut their veins. Each one of these people had worked actively during the war against the militarists and against the imperialist policy at the risk of his life. One of them had previously been sentenced to fifteen years in prison for making antiwar propaganda in the German army. He had just been freed by the revolution.

It may be said that feelings ran especially high in Aachen and that the French invasion army was particularly bitter at the beginning. The record of the British and Canadian, and also of the

United States occupation troops is different on the whole. But similar tendencies existed even among them. In a pamphlet soon to be published, Hiram Motherwell, author of The Peace We Fight For, quotes from the report of Colonel I. L. Hunt, of the American Army of Occupation in the Coblenz area, as follows: "Paragraph 5 of the Armistice was so interpreted by both Germany and the Allies that 'local' authorities meant the officials of the old regime." A decree of the Supreme Command stated that the blockade of Germany should be continued. Germany should not be permitted to buy bread even with gold until the Bolshevist menace was removed. The treatment of the German Armistice delegation in the Forest of Compiègne showed the same general attitude. The representative of the German army in this delegation, General Winterfeld, was courted; the representative of the people, the delegate of the Reichstag Peace Commission, not a Bolshevik, but a moderate Catholic, Mr. Erzberger, was snubbed. He did not belong.

This policy of dealing with the representatives of the old regime encouraged the restoration of the military gangs immediately after their defeat. The German revolution was too timid and too generous to suppress them. In the early stormy days, the populace directed their rage against officers, frequently stripping them of their epaulets. But the officer caste was only symbolically purged; it retained much of its former power.

The revenge the officers took was particularly bloody. They murdered pacifists, liberal leaders and the radicals. The long list of five hundred killed began with Erzberger, Rathenau, Eisner, Liebknecht, Luxembourg—and ended fourteen years later with the killing of the German Republic itself. Had the Allies encouraged the democratic elements instead of assisting in restoring the old guard, the history of the ensuing years would have been different.

The second example is the recent story of Italy which has important lessons for all of us. It started with political "estimates of the situation," that were fundamentally wrong. These estimates expected that Italy, after twenty years of a fascist regime, simply could have no traces of antifascism left. Before the landing in Sicily it was the general assumption that the Allies would have to fight through every village and the AMG would have to govern locally with fascist leftovers. But, instead, in every village and every town, the people hailed the armies as liberators from their fascist rulers and not merely from the Nazi gangsters. At first, this appeared to the Allied soldiers as staged. They said so. But more and more the occupation troops became convinced of the sincerity and genuineness of their reception.

The confusion in Italy, which resulted partly from a wrong political estimate of the situation and partly from the fear of "Bolshevism" as in 1918, is a mild overture to the Babylonian confusion which may develop in Germany when it is invaded. For it may turn out that the German people will act more like the Italians than the imaginary Germans envisaged in the blueprints of the experts.

Some days before Mussolini's overthrow, Italy appeared to be fascist. There were grave doubts about the existence of a second Italy. This second Italy has since come into the open. There is no doubt any more about the existence of two Frances. There were many doubts not so long ago. There is little doubt about two Yugoslavias, two Slovakias, two Rumanias. But there are still many convinced today that it will be entirely different in Germany. They are deceived by the semblance of German unity behind Hitler, which has been created by the Nazis themselves, and which has been accepted in the fear that the other Germany, should it exist, would this time definitely be a Bolshevist Germany.

It is too late now to change this misconception. Experience will teach soon, I am convinced, that among all the nations today, Germany is the most divided. The more Goebbels insists on German unity behind the cornered gangsters, the less there is really left of it. There is a Gallup Poll of blood, as evidenced by the growing lists of the executioner. And there is no inevitability of Bolshevism. Every new report from war prisoners and deserters and from inside Germany tells that in Germany today there is more fear of

Bolshevism than love for it. It is Hitler who threatens "Bolshevism," in order to terrify and confuse us. The more he is believed the more likelihood there is that National Bolshevism will arise. And that National Bolshevism may in a few years grow into a neo-Hitlerism, when the new Napoleon legend, the Hitler legend will have become strong. Today to be sure, the situation is reversed from what it was in 1933. Then, when Hitler came to power, still making use of the democratic process, he never got a majority. (He had a bare two per cent majority with the support of the reactionary Hugenberg Fronde.) At that time there were two Germanies of about equal popular strength, unequal only in power. Now, there is no equal half left for Hitler. Instead, there is fear, a guilt complex, and the naked force of the special terror troops. Even they have begun to sink into a state of demoralization.

The German rulers have long since lost the support of the old autocrats. Like Badoglio in Italy, these are already preparing to jump once more onto the bandwagon of the victors. Will it be allowed again? To work with them, to build on them has been the dream of every policy of expediency. The main trouble with an expediency policy is this: it is not expedient. Remember 1815. Remember 1918.

Once more at the crossroads of history the question must be asked: Will the German revolution be encouraged this time or will it again be *Ver-*

boten? There are doubtless certain Allied leaders who are still more afraid of the completion of the democratic revolution in Germany than they are of Hitler. But if the Allied people remember their own history, their own fight against autocracy, their own glorious revolutions, they have it in their power to write finis to German autocracy for all time to come.

II. The Dependent Revolution

WHEN Hitler came to power the active anti-Nazis in Germany vowed to overthrow him. During eleven years of cruel persecution, thousands of them have lost their lives in the ill-matched battle, more of them have gone to concentration camps and prisons, hundreds of thousands have been oppressed and silenced. But even such a decade could not destroy the hope of final victory. They felt themselves the vanguard of German democracy. They knew they had lost a battle. They knew they would win the next battle. They knew the Hitler Reich was only a setback in the long-term fight for democracy—maybe the last serious setback on the hard path to the definite establishment of militant democracy.

There is an old German workers' song whose words have lived on in the hearts of millions of the pre-Hitler labor movement, in spite of the humiliating defeat: ". . . friends, we shall return stronger than ever before." In the years of deepest depression before the war, when it seemed that Hitler had wiped out all resistance in Germany,

and had conquered for an indefinite time to come,
those courageous anti-Nazis who were still carrying on the fight, often felt that they were trying
to empty the ocean with a teaspoon. For the outside world seemed reconciled to Hitler and was
helping him to build golden bridges to further
conquests. They were confused by the fact that
many, too many, Germans had been infected by
the Hitler poison. But, even then, there were
groups in Germany who were confident that international changes would create new opportunities
for the anti-Nazi revolution. Then the soul of the
lost people would be won back and their integrity
would be restored. When England and France
declared war on Hitler Germany the vague hopes
of the past took on new life. Here was the first
definite prospect that a chance to defeat the Nazis
would come within a reasonable time. In spite of
Hitler's initial series of lightning victories, hopes
grew steadily as the war continued.

Now the world has changed.

Now the days of Hitler's rule are numbered.
One fascist regime has already crumbled. Soon
the Nazis will follow their Italian friends. Gradually, in outline, appear the contours of the world
which is to replace Hitler's. And now, for the first
time, it is evident that during the long years since
Hitler seized power German anti-Nazis have clung
to certain illusions in an effort to make their
existence bearable. One of these is the illusion that
a democratic spring will follow close on the Hitler

winter. But history is not written in such simple terms. Only now is it possible to understand how grave was the defeat suffered by progressive forces in Germany and how great are the damages for which post-Hitler Germany will have to pay. In the tragic fate of the Italian people there is some indication of the things to come for post-Hitler Germany. After the military defeat total party rule will be followed by total collapse. The ensuing upheaval will be a revolution in shackles, a dependent revolution and although there will be spontaneous revolutionary outbreaks there will be no organized democratic leadership ready to take command immediately.

There will be forces of freedom in Germany. They will come out into the open just as in Italy, where they proved to be surprisingly strong after twenty years of oppression. But for many of the Italian anti-fascists who came out of hiding and out of the prisons when Mussolini was ousted, the first revolutionary demonstrations resulted in new persecutions and death. A longer time may elapse in Germany than in Italy before the forces of freedom, the democratic anti-Nazis, will be able to bring the revolt born in dependence to independent fulfillment. The clearer the vision of a new democratic leadership for Germany, the sooner the democratic revolution will be fulfilled and a revolutionary democracy established.

Why will this be dependent revolution? The anti-Nazi revolution will be circumscribed for an indefinite period by international controls. It will be dependent on the military and administrative measures of the victorious powers. Some of the anti-Nazis have always known that the only chance for liberation from National Socialism would come with a German military defeat. They were aware of the terrible dangers of Nazism years before people who now attack them for having done "nothing effective to stop Hitler or to start a revolution." * Revolutions cannot be "started" when you want them. They come in their own time, according to their own laws, most of them after military defeats of despotic powers. And that is why they are nearly always dependent on forces from outside, on their military conquerors. It is impossible to forsee how little freedom the coming German revolution will have when its time arrives —at the outset it will be almost totally dependent on outside forces.

Every deep-rooted change in Germany is necessarily beset by certain difficulties because of Germany's dependence on other countries, her lack of basic raw materials, and her geographical position in the center of the Europeon continent. This is one of the reasons why German revolutions until now have never been successful. It is a vicious circle. German revolutions have always been delayed and retarded. Their leadership has always been weak and Europe has never been

---

* *Lessons of My Life*, by Rt. Hon. Lord Robert Vansittart. Knopf, New York, 1943, p. 86.

mature enough to tolerate or to protect a German revolution. By the end of the war, after the extensive destruction of German productive machinery, Germany will be more dependent than ever. She will be more helpless because of her acute scarcity problem and because her economic industrialization and centralization were intensified by the war. There will be an additional reason for Germany's post-war dependence transcending all the others in importance. After the defeat of Hitler, Germany's existence as a nation will be at stake. Powerful groups among the United Nations are concerned less with the liberation, or the democratization of the German people, than with drastic measures they believe to be necessary in order to eliminate German aggression forever. The hatred unloosed by Hitler's barbarism will demand a complete destruction of the German Reich. Such a solution, for example, is presented by Lord Vansittart, former Under-Secretary of the Foreign Office. Vansittart's supporters will offer his "Four Prerequisites" instead of Franklin Roosevelt's Four Freedoms, namely, "defeat, demilitarization, occupation, re-education. . . ." Vansittart believes that without these the Four Freedoms will be "moonshine." *

Democratic Germany, as the heir of Hitler, will be faced by the most severe trials. In the chapters to follow, the new and unique problems that will be raised in the coming change are to be analyzed.

* *Ibid.,* p. **xxi.**

They include: (1) The limitations placed on the revolution by foreign intervention. (2) The nature of the forces for freedom that will emerge in spite of obstacles. (3) Germany's international position after two lost wars. (4) And, finally, the chief problem—that of creating new democratic movements to perpetuate the traditions of the historical democratic movements, especially the traditions of the German labor movement, under a new leadership and after an interruption of more than eleven years, and thus to bring peace and freedom to Germany at last.

The first chapters of the story beginning with Hitler's defeat can be written in advance. No extraordinary gift of prophesy is necessary as they are the logical continuation of trends already started.

During the fifth winter of war, after nearly three years of a war of attrition in the East, the symptoms of the declining strength of the German war regime were evident. Gradually the Nazis had been driven on to the defensive. They had lost great battles, Stalingrad, Tunis, Sicily and Italy, and finally had been forced into the general retreat from the Ukraine. They were retiring from the outer bastions of their "fortress Europe" to the inner fortress Germany. For months they had not been in a position to put up effective defense against paralyzing air offensives that had brought ruin to great parts of western and northern Ger-

many and that finally had even reached the once
protected areas in the south and center of the
country. Scarcities of all sorts, which had been only
temporarily alleviated during the period of blitz,
had become steadily worse, in spite of control of
all of conquered Europe's industries and land.
The evacuation of the conquests had already begun. The most serious obstacles in the way of the
Nazis regaining the initiative were inadequate
labor and troop reserves. The European Axis had
been politically dismembered; it had started when
Mussolini had been reduced to puppet head of
an exiled Italian government, shaking the confidence of the smaller vassal states in Berlin. As
a result of these setbacks and defeats, the final
crisis had indeed begun while "three hundred
powerful German divisions" were still intact. German superiority in the scattered points on the
fronts where it still existed could not survive long
after the Allies were finally able to supplement
their secondary fronts and their terrific air offensives with a real second front on the European
continent. It may well be that the German military power will have crumbled or surrendered by
the time this book is published.

If there is doubt when and how the "untenable"
fortress will surrender, there is no longer any
doubt that it will. After the successful Badoglio
plot to overthrow Mussolini in Italy, the Nazis
had to play their last trump card on the home
front. Himmler and the S. S. took over with the

battle cry "there is no way back." The Nazi party regime dug in in the last trench of self-defense, still a gangster but already a cornered one. Passive resistance to the war was growing in great sections of the people. There had even been riots and strikes. There were reversals of policy, political purges of military leaders as well as the "soft-hearted" or "cowardly" Nazis. Important new commando posts were taken over by party functionaries; the powers of the Gauleiters were expanded to make them all-powerful commissars; additional control was extended over war industries, which formerly enjoyed a certain amount of "industrial self-government"; terror became increasingly severe; the executioner worked overtime killing people convicted simply of "defeatism." The base of National Socialism in German life was shrinking fast. Under the surface the number of forces who were ready to surrender was growing rapidly. Goebbels tried then to impress on the German people that their choice was between fighting to the bitter end with the Nazis, and being subjected to unspeakable brutalities by their conquerors. To prove his thesis Goebbels' propaganda high-lighted proposals and threats made in the United Nations which, he hoped, would strike terror to the hearts of the German people. But he could not restore the broken morale. Painful as the prospects envisaged for Germany by certain groups among the Allies were, an increasing number of Germans preferred them to the endless terror of Nazi war. More and more realized that the war was hopelessly lost.

Therefore, it can be taken for granted, that this crisis which has indeed started will soon come into the open. Whether the situation analogous to the one which produced the Badoglio coup d'état in Italy is more apt in Germany to lead first to a palace revolution or a revolution from below, cannot be predicted with certainty. However, in Germany as was the case in Italy, it is unlikely that a popular uprising shortening the war significantly will have occurred before the end. It is much more likely that the chief expression of the dissatisfaction of the masses of the people will be confined to growing passive resistance, hastening the coming of the defeat by weakening the economy and, in this way, the military power of Hitler's defense. More highly developed revolutionary movements will gain momentum in the very last period before the collapse. They may be able to develop only as the military defense is collapsing. Thus, military factors primarily will determine the time and the immediate circumstances of the defeat.

Grave losses, mounting deterioration of Germany's productive forces, swelling passive resistance and, especially, the growing military might of the Allies will usher in the final crisis of the Nazi regime. In the revolution connected with the defeat, the familiar appurtenances of past revolutions as we have known them—the independent uprising of the oppressed classes, the seizure of power by their leaders, the ousting of their old rulers—will be present only in embryo if at all. Any *independent* beginnings of this nature prior to an Allied occupation will hardly be able to prevent the occupation itself. The disarmament of the Nazis, demobilization, the punishment of the war criminals, the beginning of reconstruction, the birth of democratic bodies, will then take place only with the encouragement or at least the tolerance of the victors. In this respect and only in this respect the course of events in Germany will bear more similarity to the French Restoration after Napoleon than to the revolt of 1918 in Germany, although this "November revolt" was also dependent on the victors. It has recently been the fashion to study the Restoration in France following Napoleon, and to praise the Peace of the Holy Alliance as an example of how to calm a deeply revolutionized aggressor nation. This study can give but little enlightenment for future treatment of Germany. First, it is certainly not true that the Congress of Vienna brought lasting peace to Europe, above all it did not calm France. By 1823, only nine years after Waterloo, France had invaded Spain. She was in constant inner convulsions. Twenty-five years after Napoleon's defeat France was again an interventionist power of the first order. Before 1870, she had been primarily responsible for launching five wars. They were: the counterrevolutionary expedition in Spain, the intervention against the Roman Republic in 1849, the Crimean War in 1854, the war with Piedmont against Austria in 1859, the Mexican expedition in 1861. The "peace" of 1815 is an example of how not to achieve lasting peace. Second, it is still more confusing to find people today searching for modern "Fouchés" and "Talleyrands" in Hitler's entourage. For nearly half a century, Europe was spoiled and sick as a result of the reactionary coalition under the leadership of Metternich and the Czar. Whatever similarities there may be, and we have pointed some of them out, they should certainly keep us from trying to repeat the sorrows of the *experience Talleyrand*. In any case, the general outlines of the character of the coming anti-Hitler revolt in Germany can therefore be foreseen only after an analysis of its own component elements. It may well start as did the Italian revolt in July 1943. Its channels may be even more thoroughly choked than were those of the revolutionary movements of Rome, Milan, Turin and for a longer period.

TOTAL ECONOMIC COLLAPSE

The downfall of Hitler's European system will have repercussions without parallel in history. The collapse of Italy was scarcely an overture, nor can this cataclysm be compared with 1918. The German collapse of 194— as compared with that of 1918 will be like the crashing down of a skyscraper built on sand as compared with the cracking of the walls of a solidly built house whose foundations remain unshaken. The victors will undoubtedly try to institute emergency preventive measures, to avert a complete collapse that would involve all Europe in hardship and chaos, even endangering the victors. It is not certain whether the victors can agree on common measures, whether they will have the vision and the means necessary to take preventive steps or whether they will act in time. Therefore, those factors whose combined effect will mean total collapse of the economy of Germany and most of Europe unless means are found and put into effect to prevent it, must be enumerated.

First, the greatest economic shock will be the cessation of all of Europe's war industries. As Nazi Europe's economy was geared primarily to war production, the defeat will necessarily bring the major part of industry on the continent to a full stop. In Germany proper that will mean that most of the approximately sixteen million Germans and foreigners—men, women and young children—who worked in the war industries will suddenly be unemployed. No matter how quickly the Allied authorities begin, the reconstruction of a peacetime economy will require complicated preparations that will take months and even years. A continuation of some war production in Europe for Allied purposes, such as, prosecuting the war in the Far East, may mitigate conditions, but its total effect will be slight.

Second, there will be a tendency toward both vertical and horizontal dismemberment of the highly centralized economic machinery developed by the Nazis. This will interrupt production in non-war industries if the collapse follows its free course. Vertical dismemberment will be caused by the inevitable dissolution of the central administrative and control organs of Nazi economy through the removal of leading officials, and directors and Industry Group Leaders. As the higher economic officials are Nazis in Germany, and are collaborationists in the occupied countries, a decapitation of the leadership of Nazi economy can hardly be hindered and must not be hindered. But replacement of even a part of this personnel will present all kinds of difficulties, even if the victors bring trained economic administrators in the train of their armies as the Germans did when they entered France and other countries. Even if skilled personnel is available, changes in the administration will cause serious dislocation.

Horizontal dismemberment of the European economy now centralized in Germany will automatically follow the national uprisings of the oppressed peoples, military occupation and the establishment of new military fronts. The Nazi war economy apparatus not only concentrated the raw material and labor supply from all of Europe in the German center, it also did the reverse. It took new industry to great marginal areas in districts protected from air raids. Among the districts involved are Upper Silesia, the Czech "Protectorate," and certain reconstructed Polish industrial areas around Lodz and Warsaw. All these districts, including those which are German, will probably be cut off at once and this will mean a further mutilation of the German production apparatus, involving the loss not only of raw materials, but also of semi-manufactured goods and power plants that formerly fed the German industrial center. The experience of 1918 showed that such changes bring powerful disturbances.

Third, the entire artificial system of fixed prices and wages, of controlled exchanges and rationing will break down when the central authority is overthrown. With the hunger that will prevail at the end of this war and the mass impoverishment which the war has already caused, there will be desperate fighting over every crust of bread.

Fourth, Germany's old dependence on raw materials from outside, especially, iron, raw textiles, and food stuffs, will reassert itself immediately. The lack of raw materials will, moreover, cause further stoppages in the new synthetic industries. Although some of the ersatz industries developed by the Nazis, including a part of the artificial fibers, synthetic oil, and plastic industries, will survive the collapse, the raw material scarcity must severely affect even these chemical industries. They are based on coal and wood. Already Germany's coal industry is particularly hard hit, many plants have been destroyed by air raids, and in the mines there is a high percentage of over-aged and foreign workers. Even with the products of Polish, Belgian and French mines at their disposal, Germany is already suffering from a coal deficit. The separation of these areas from Germany will greatly increase the shortage. In addition, the large imports of wood from the occupied countries for ersatz industries will be cut off at once, and those industries affected, especially synthetic fiber, will close down. The Allies may not permit the synthetic oil production to continue.

Fifth, there will be chaos in the labor market. The overwhelming majority of the more than ten million foreign workers cannot be held in Germany, in spite of any restrictions that may be imposed. They will start out, and, if necessary, fight their way home. With foreign workers leaving Germany and German troops marching home there will be mass migrations. Germany's skilled labor stock will shrink to a few millions. The departure of foreign workers will lighten Germany's own unemployment problem, but there will be millions too few jobs for the soldiers returning home and for the workers of Germany. And there will be the special unemployment problem of the dissolved Nazi bureaucracy, the hundreds of thousands of members of the disbanded S. S. and the police troops and the lower employees of the state and party—those not killed during the revolt.

In comparison with this unemployment problem, that of 1918, the most trying of the demobilization problems of that time, seems rather minor.

Sixth, the obsolescence of machines and destruction by air raids will have created unbearable conditions in the industrial centers, especially in western Germany. There will have been more destruction during this war in German industries than in all the other areas of destruction together. The last battles and the civil war that may take place in Germany itself will add other devastated areas, and there will be no machines and no raw materials for immediate reconstruction.

Seventh, there will be chaos in public and private property ownership. There will be not only the problem of purely party institutions, like the Labor Front plants and the Hermann Goering Works, but the entire question of the property that formerly belonged to German Jewish people and to foreigners, and of the penetration of German trusts and the German state into foreign enterprise during the war. In short, all the property which has been directly or indirectly expropriated by the Nazis will have to be untangled.

Most of these problems existed in a lesser form in Italy too. There were industrial regions in Italy in which production stopped completely after the collapse. Supplies of all kinds were blocked, and the people were starving. But the disaster in Italy, still primarily an agricultural country, cannot be compared with the over-all disaster which will come to industrial and over-bureaucratized Germany.

Even this rough picture of the predictable factors indicates such turmoil, confusion and dislocation in the entire economy, that it can only be described as total collapse.

DISSOLUTION OF THE PARTY STATE

For twenty years the world did not know what an anti-fascist revolution would look like, what resistance the all-powerful party regime would present in its final hour. There has been a suspicion that the fascist resilience might last to the very end, that not only a few regiments of "black hundreds," such as those who tried to defend the tottering throne of the Czar in 1917, but many divisions, black hundred thousands of S. S. men might fight for every corner of the fascist fortress.

But no, the outstanding surprise in the night and the day which followed Mussolini's arrest by Badoglio's handful of police officers was the complete lack of a last-ditch defense by the faithful Praetorians. The entire nation boiled up after it heard the news. Millions and millions walked out in the streets of Italy unarmed. In Rome itself, hundreds of thousands, some in pajamas, gathered before the famous balcony of the Palazzia Venezia from which the noisy dictator had harangued the people year after year. They were in a delirium

of joy, scolding and ridiculing the bogey of yesterday. It does not minimize the significance of the
revolution that these millions in Turin, in Milan,
all over Italy, were unable, in the coming weeks,
to get rid of the new usurper of power, the old
fox, Badoglio. They were threatened by invasion
from two sides. They had obviously no organization, no known and authoritative leadership.
They broke down what little was left of army
morale, and paralyzed attempts to drive them back
with the threat of guns and tanks. They besieged
the few local defenders of the fascists in offices,
newspaper buildings and their private villas. Unarmed and unorganized as they were, they forced
the fascists to surrender. Not even the Nazi invaders' intervention in the north could revive
the broken-down party regime's authority. Bloody
battles had to be fought against these popular
defenders of liberation and German troops had
to take over.

In the face of the threat of two interventions,
parts of the state apparatus, namely the prefec-
tures, police troops, and the Bersaglieri, were
able to retain some traditional local control. But
not the fascist party. It had no defenders at all!

In Sicily and southern Italy where the AMG
offered the local fascist authorities an opportunity
to stay in their jobs, most of them ran away. They
disappeared, and *nolens volens* the occupying
military government had to take ordinary citizens
as their first collaborators. A regime has never

crumbled so suddenly. Indeed, it exploded into dust!

How will it be in Germany?

It will not be so fundamentally different. There have been some interesting hints of news to come. Badoglio, in his first interview with Allied newspapermen, revealing details of Mussolini's fall from power, mentioned also a significant item about the state of mind of the Germans. "He [Badoglio] said, that when Mussolini's regime collapsed, unfounded rumors that Hitler had been assassinated swept 'all the German soldiers in Rome into ecstasies of joy.' " *

Ecstasies of joy, that is what German soldiers expressed at the first performance. And that, in spite of the fact that Hitler's regime has had less time thoroughly to discredit itself, one decade in place of two for Mussolini. The Italian youth had become completely disgusted with the fascism that had once seduced them. Will it be so different with German youth? There are differences; for example, when Mussolini's party exploded his military power had already been annihilated; German military power is not yet broken. Some survival of the myth of its one-time invincibility may act as a retarding influence even in the hour of its final defeat. Also, the Italian people knew that they were not fighting for survival. In spite of the slogan of unconditional surrender, it was

* New York *Times*, October 5, 1943.

absolutely clear that their chances could only improve if they deserted the Axis.

These are important differences. They will prolong the resistance of Nazi Germany as a whole. But will the Nazi party, finally cornered, come out any better in the end?

Certainly it will not. There are even some conditions in Germany favorable to the collapse of the Nazi party, for which there was no analogy in Italy. Eleven years of Hitler have not so completely liquidated the democratic traditions of the previous regime among the older generation. German youth may not be as advanced as the Italian youth, but that disadvantage is balanced by more surviving democrats in the pre-Hitler generations. In Germany the army of more than ten million enemy aliens, of foreign workers and war prisoners will contribute to disintegration. The most demoralizing factor of all is the Germans' awareness that they are fighting alone, that they are hopelessly encircled. Thus, Hitler's party will go to pieces like Mussolini's. It remains only a question of time.

It is possible that final AMG plans for Germany will try to include parts of the Nazi machine, particularly the economic machine, in its transitional emergency system. But it is practically impossible, in spite of fear of revolutionary developments and in spite of the appeasement tendencies of certain circles among the Allies, that the occupation authorities will back or even

tolerate any *vital* section of the political apparatus
of the Nazis. Political control has been concentrated increasingly in the hands of a narrow circle
of higher party functionaries and of the S. S. If
the Allies should attempt to carry on some part
of the Reich administration with so-called "moderate Nazis," even these could not prevent the
complete liquidation of the party machine after
the military defeat. When defeat has robbed the
Nazi leaders of control over the military machine
and the police, when the economic collapse has
liquidated their administrative centers, it is most
improbable that the real force behind the regime
today, the home front divisions of the S. S., will
have any strength remaining.

The power of the Nazis rested not only on their
civil war and terror machines but also on the
voluntary support of millions of adherents and the
semi-voluntary or forced support of oppressed
sections of the population. A defeat of such dimensions, the discrediting of all the Nazis' ideologies,
their glory and their hopes, will have taken the
masses of voluntary supporters away from the
Nazis, and have moved to action other masses,
who hitherto had not gone beyond passive resistance. The party mechanism will not be able
to survive such a blow. It cannot expect fighting
to the last even on the part of fanatically devoted
S. S. divisions.

Their last fight is on now! The only difference
from Italy—a difference deriving primarily from

the comparatively greater strength of Germany—
is that after years of preparing for the armed
security of the regime, the resistance of despera-
tion kept Hitler from collapsing at the time when
the Italian convulsion shook the Nazi foundations.
"We have just skirted an abyss," Goebbels said
afterwards. But this resistance can hardly be successful over a long period or in a broad area. The
party rule will collapse if only a part of its chief
apparatus is liquidated. An active and fanatic core
of the Nazi movement may seek survival underground.

Thus, the rapid growth of opposition in the
final period and the sudden disintegration of the
Nazi machine during the collapse will reduce the
power of the Nazis, just as the fascists' power was
reduced in Italy. A special characteristic of this
revolution will be that the familiar processes will
be delayed and then compressed into a brief final
phase. Every revolution has a latent period of
preparation, and its organs develop slowly long
before the actual uprising. In the case of the anti-
Nazi revolution, the revolutionary organs will not
develop until the acute, final crisis. This crisis
will have an even more explosive character than
the Italian. Therefore, even an intermission with
a German Badoglio can be only a short one. It is
lack of imagination which makes people believe,
as many do, that a more or less stable army regime
will most probably follow immediately after Hitler. The German army after Hitler may hold

together somewhat better than the Italian army after Mussolini. The difference will be only relative, not decisive. It can be kept together only by support from outside, if the Allies should choose to make units of the beaten German army a policing agent.

The possible role of the army will be clear from a comparison with 1918. Then the army initiated the change in the regime and requested that the democratic and labor groups take over. But the army could maneuver this change only on the basis of the existing democratic institutions. The regime of the Kaiser, with its parliament and its war constitution, never robbed the political parties, the trade unions and other class organizations of *all* their rights and liberties during the war, even during the time of the most intensive state intervention. The activities of their organizations were curtailed, but the organizations themselves were not dissolved. Thus they could form the nucleus for the opposition. When the collapse came the state executive remained practically intact in spite of the military defeats. Hindenburg and his generals led the defeated armies home in a more or less orderly manner. The soldiers' councils that grew up at this time were often only the regrouped former leaders of army units. Genuine revolts and mutinies were limited to a few acute situations such as the sailors' revolt in Kiel and later the "Soviets" in Bremen and Munich. It was not till later, after the troops had already arrived home, that additional revolts flared up. The administration and the centers of the war economy continued to function. They were not in a position to reorganize production, but during the transitional period they did supply important machinery for maintaining order and dissolving the government control of the war economy. A part of the actual authority for keeping order was in the hands of the trade unions, whose leaders had penetrated into the manpower and labor agencies during the war. On the basis of a joint committee with the leaders of industry that was organized during the spring of 1918 and began to function during the days of the revolution, the unions became the most important mass basis for the new regime. The Reichstag groups of the Social Democratic and Catholic oppositions and their parliamentary committees were the centers of negotiation for the transitional government. In other words, organs which had grown up within the old social structure—expanded into democratic mass organizations, and with new representative bodies, such as factory councils—took on the functions of liquidating the war. The Allied armies halted at the boundaries of Germany, only frontier districts were occupied. There was no military intervention in the heart of Germany.

In the coming revolution it is not likely that there will be an equivalent of Hindenburg leading intact units of the army complete with officers, much as the Moscow Free Germany Committee

might count on such an eventuality. Nor will
there be administrative centers that continue to
function. Nor will there be any experienced
democratic organs of the opposition. Unless the
U.S.S.R. or the Allies jointly decide to use most
of the present party, the present personnel, the
present criminals, the existing body politic of
Germany will dissolve just as Mussolini's did.

Once the cohesion of the ruling strata of the
party state is dissolved, German society will be
completely atomized. Administrative and executive branches of the government—which are
organs of the National Socialist party—will fall
apart. In other sectors of society, the story will
be much the same. In the Economic Groups and
Industry Groups of the bureaucratic apparatus
into which the Nazis have divided all business,
industry, and agriculture, most of the leaders are
Nazis, but even those who are not party members
are privileged beneficiaries of the war and of the
Nazi party. Some of the lowest units may survive
after separating themselves entirely from the
broken system. For example, village units of the
Reich Farm Estate may in some instances emerge
after the cataclysm as democratic nuclei. The
same may be true of some minor branches of a less
important industry group. But these, even if they
are not completely atomized, will be impotent,
having been torn from their former parent organizations. Cartellized industries will supply a certain organizing force, especially those which had

international contacts before the war, some of which have been maintained. However, the community of interest within the cartels will not be adequate to supply a real resistance to, or place a brake on, the general liquidation tendencies. Many of the subordinate business and government administrative bodies in the occupied territories will be cut off just as suddenly as the local industries or the hemmed-in armies. The ruins of the Nazi state, the gigantic machine that extended over all Europe, will be pressed together within the territory of the former Weimar Republic.

As the opposition had to exist underground entirely, the nuclei of the new movement could not develop beyond the narrowest circles. These democratic beginnings will be strong enough to achieve *local* authority here and there during the period of revolution, to organize factory committees and to set up village security units. They may set up party committees like the six-party committee in Milan, but they will scarcely be able to create a provisional government immediately, and the least desirable government is a puppet government. In the 1917 revolution in Russia, it took almost half a year before a network of Soviets was joined into the first national congress. And in Russia there were remnants of democratic organizations and intervention from outside did not come until later. When the Allied armies, however, did intervene in Russia, though their forces were not large, they overthrew Soviet power temporarily in every district except the provinces of Moscow and Petersburg.

The recent Italian experience is even more enlightening. The Italian people, suddenly freed of the hypnosis of the fascist state power after Mussolini's overthrow, were strong enough to clean up their little local Mussolinis. But, though they fought heroically, they were weaker than the German invaders and there was no question of resisting other outside intervention.

Is there in Germany an apparatus similar to the one Badoglio used during his forty days of rule? Again, the police, the regional and local government administrations in Germany are more completely coordinated in the Nazi system, than the comparable institutions in Italy were in the fascist system. In Germany there have been no centers where the seeds of freedom have existed as in some of the Italian villages, in the regional administrations and in the universities. The only non-National Socialist organizations which have remained in Germany—they too as the prisoners of the Nazis—are the churches. It is possible that in the last stages of preparation before the revolution some church organizations will serve as preliminary starting points of revolt. In fascist Italy, as in Czarist Russia and Nazi Germany, church processions and church services have sometimes taken on a demonstratively political character. But the churches cannot replace all the other missing social centers and become the organizing

force for the mass movement during the days of
revolution. Also, within the church hierarchies
there are bitter conflicts. Intransigent anti-Nazi
wings, like the Niemoeller group in the Protes-
tant, and the Faulhaber-von Gahlen group in the
Catholic Church, as well as a part of the lower
clergy, are involved in a struggle for leadership
with the appeasers within their organizations. The
Catholic majority of greater Germany will be
transformed back again into a minority in smaller
Germany, and the Protestants are not united
among themselves. The lack of unity among the
denominations will lessen the central influence of
the churches. Moreover, the churches will not
want to be exponents of revolutionary movements
which might threaten their religious authority. In
so far as the churches act politically, they will be a
conservative, retarding force; some of their most
intransigent anti-Nazis, such as Faulhaber, are at
the same time, their most die-hard reactionaries.
As in Italy, there will be strong differentiation between hierarchy and lower clergy. The churches
will move away from the Nazis. They will certainly not defend them; but neither will they be
the leaders of the liberation.

It can be predicted, therefore, that the Nazi regime, once having fallen, will find no defender,
but that the liberated masses will have no democratic organs, at least none that will exercise national authority. A German Badoglio regime supported by the victorious powers is not impossible

as a short term expediency, but it would certainly
not be democratic. It would not have the support
or the mandate of a large section of the German
people. Even the still faithful part of the Hitler
Youth and the S.S. will not be able to withstand
the pressure of the collapse. A part of the youth
will have been annihilated in the war. (According
to rough estimates, by the end of 1943, out of
about five million young men of 17-25, at least
two million had been killed and about a million
others had been crippled.) A part will have been
taken prisoners, and another part will dissociate
itself from the shattered Nazi regime. Of the tens
of thousands of younger leaders of the party, and
younger S.S. members many will have been killed
along with the Nazi Old Guard by the Allies or in
the first popular outburst; others will try to escape. Meanwhile, the first local organs of self-government will be struggling to get started. They
will be very weak at the beginning, committees
hastily formed in local communities by liberated
political prisoners, men and women from underground circles and members of factory councils.
During the period of revolution, the active par-
ticipants in the movement will be mostly workers,
probably many of them foreign conscript workers.
Movements that spring up under such circumstances tend to be negative in their immediate
aspirations, particularly bitter toward the former
tyrants and against continuing foreign wars. Beyond such negative objectives, the new movement

will scarcely have a clear program, developed plans, or advanced organizations. We may expect that surviving representatives of the old labor movement will have a greater authority than others in the mass movements and in the new party committees at the beginning. Furthermore, it is possible that neo-communist forces in the labor movement may have a stronger position than any others for a time. This may be a difference from Italy, where the communist movement had never broken the monopoly of the socialists in the great industrial centers. However, the lasting influence of neo-communist groups will largely depend in a negative or affirmative sense on the methods of the occupation and on the peace conditions the Allies impose, and especially on those of the Soviet Union.

A New Shortage: Leaders for Freedom

The most important weakness of the revolution under the conditions we have described, will be its lack of experienced and recognized democratic leadership at the outset. Inevitably, once total party rule is removed, social revolutionary forces and mass movements driving towards freedom will be released. But the economic collapse we have described and foreign intervention will make it very difficult to organize for freedom. There has been more than a ten year interruption in the continuity of democratic organization in Germany, with no democratic education or political training of any kind for the masses. Moreover, Germany has a special tradition of weakness in democratic leadership. Therefore, the ability of the German people to rule themselves and to cope with problems, such as will exist in a period of revolutionary change will be greatly impaired. But, at the same time, the German people will have learned a profound lesson from two lost wars and the bitter experience of party dictatorship.

National Socialism began as a counter-revolutionary force directed against the labor movement. The aim of Nazi terror was to eradicate all potential democratic leadership. The successfully prosecuted policy of destroying democratic organizations and leaders was an essential part of the preparation for an imperialist war. The war itself has called forth international forces which will defeat the German war machine, but which also contain tendencies that will impede the development of an independent democratic leadership for Germany. These tendencies are not the definitive and uniform policy of Allied leadership. Among the United Nations there are variations in policy and intent in accordance with different interests, varying degrees of fear, variations that correspond with the shifts in the relation of forces within the Allied coalition. The longer the war lasts, the greater the sacrifices, and the more extensive the destruction, the stronger will be the tendency toward a "hard," dictated and drastic peace, directed not only against the German war machine but also against democratic self-determination by the German people. Chauvinistic ideologies emerge, and not only among the small victim nations; they are growing also in certain groups within the great powers. Nourished by reactionary interests, a kind of reversed racism is developing in specific circles among the Allies.

People have forgotten, and in increasing numbers of late, that Hitler fought Germany first for fourteen years before he achieved power there. It has passed unnoticed that growing sections of the German people have endured the continuation of Nazi rule and the war unwillingly and passively. Expectations for revolt in Germany, grossly exaggerated by many journalists a number of years ago, sank again to nothing. Because of their impotence, German anti-Nazis have lost almost all their credit abroad. This has not been fundamentally changed by the sudden appointment of some German communist refugees to the Moscow Free Germany Committee. We shall discuss this committee later; it should be said, however, that the central figure of this committee is not the old communist exile, but the young German officer war prisoner. Not only the interruption in the continuity of the democratic movements for more than a decade, but also increasingly reactionary tendencies in the war leadership of some of the Allied countries today hinder preparations for a democratic change in Germany. Even if these tendencies become milder as Hitler Germany grows weaker and because of an Allied compromise, they will still be strong enough to impose considerable limitations on the democratic character of the revolution.

Therefore, if it is permissible to count on a certain readiness of the masses for activity, to count on their having some experience and a general idea of freedom from memories of the past and as a reaction to the Nazi rule, it is permissible also to count on *inadequacy and backwardness in their leadership*. The leadership for a democratic revolution needs more thorough and more careful preparation than do the people themselves. But all the difficulties named will hinder the maturation of just that leadership. The underground movement in Germany was cut down to a very narrow circle of the younger and more active members of the old democratic parties. The disparity between the political strength of this group and the responsibilities of preparing for and leading a people's government under the most trying conditions is very great. It is not known to what extent the underground movement in Germany is maturing and increasing its contacts now. It is indicative that heretofore no single document from an inside group setting forth a clear program and clear aims has reached the outer world.

Though the manifesto of the Munich students cannot be considered as an exception, because it does not even pretend to be a program, it is of special symptomatic interest. Written and circulated underground after Hitler's first disastrous defeat at Stalingrad, it is indicative of a new trend among the German intelligentsia. After its publication the educated classes were singled out for special, bitter attack by Goebbels. The Munich statement was drawn up by students and soldiers following an incident in January, 1943, when a Nazi Gauleiter insulted women students at a university meeting. It is more than a protest against a petty Nazi official, it is a declaration of principle. "The day of reckoning has come, the day of reckoning of our German youth with the most despicable tyranny under which our people has ever suffered. . . . We demand that Adolf Hitler's state give back to us the most precious possession of the German people which he stole from us—our personal liberty. . . . Our interest is in true scholarship and in genuine freedom of spirit. No threats can frighten us, even threats of closing our universities. Everyone of us is fighting for his future, for his liberty and his honor in a state which will recognize its moral obligation." A translation of the full text of the manifesto will be found in the Appendix.

It is a document of a spiritual rebellion among "Hitler's children." The student bodies in German universities are limited to the scions of respectable families, young men and women who come from the sector of German society which followed Hitler after the defeat of German democracy. This manifesto, which asked for a boycott of Nazi teaching and of the Nazi party, and appealed to European youth to rise against the new Napoleon, and which led to the death sentences for its young German authors, is evidence of the beginning of an anti-Nazi change in the very heart of former German nationalism. It is evidence of a process, slow in starting, that is essentially similar to what took place in Italy. It was delayed because the control the Nazis exerted in intellectual life was more vigorous than that which the fascists exerted. In Italy, there was relative freedom of debate in the *litorale,* the debating seminars at the universities which had no analogy in the "barrack yard" universities of the Third Reich. People were relatively free to read books all through the fascist period, and there was no counterpart of the zealous and dogmatic book burning pyres erected by Goebbels. The change has been slower in coming in Germany too, because German intellectuals were more seriously poisoned than were the Italians under the more liberal fascist influences. However, the importance of what is happening in Germany now, the fact that German students and some professors are digging into the ideologies of liberation of a century ago as in the student manifesto and beginning to think independently, should not be exaggerated. It does not mean that a mature leadership for a coming democratic revolution is being reproduced underground. It signifies a change in the intellectual section of the mid-

dle classes. It is a first swallow on the horizon and
not yet the summer. It is of great potential importance, but not a sign of actual strength.

Numerous recent reports, some that have leaked
out through underground channels, some from
statements of German prisoners of war, tell of a
general flaring up of the classic anti-Nazi underground movement, the labor movement. There
are reports about "red regiments" in the German
army, units recruited from concentration camps,
turned into shock troops, when the manpower
crisis forced the Nazi to risk using proven "sub-
versive" elements. There are other reports about
the reactivization of underground contacts, local
groups, even large organizations. The underground workers' movement in one important
northern industrial city was wiped out in 1935,
its leaders were sent to prisons and concentration
camps; in 1939 with the outbreak of the war,
formerly active members back from the concentration camp, started to build the group again and
developed it into a much larger and much better
adjusted unit than ever before. Indeed, it is known
that by the fall of 1943 many industrial sections of
Germany were pretty well undermined by an elaborate network of local underground groups. Here
again Germany is going the Italian way. In Italy
the new anti-fascist groups date from the period
after 1934, their development paralleled the imperialistic adventures of Mussolini. Their flowering came with the disappearance of the fascist

military myth, in Spain, in Greece, finally in Africa. Following this pattern, the new German underground development is young, it is merely beginning. Still comparatively weak, it is far from maturity. The last period as Hitler's power declines may accelerate this slow-motion process. It would, nevertheless, be wishful thinking to expect the new anti-Nazi society to mature to perfection under cover of the last desperate defense of the Nazis. The air war itself destroys with equal effectiveness Nazi authority and the stability of the underground network. In the north, for example, evacuated city populations wandering the German roads to new asylums are hotbeds of grumbling, but not the best material for a growth of democratic cadres.

The German anti-Nazi emigrants abroad are especially poorly equipped to provide help for the democratic revolution after Hitler. Numerically, by far the greater part of the contemporary emigration from Germany is not a political emigration at all, but is made up of refugees from anti-Semitic persecution, most of them middle-class business and professional people. Exiles of the German labor movement in former periods played more important roles than in the present; they formed connecting links during periods when the normal functioning of the labor movement was interrupted. In the persecution under Bismarck, during the ten years of the so-called (anti-) "Socialist Law," the young German labor movement was not only able to publish its newspapers and some other literature abroad and to smuggle it systematically into the country, but was able to hold party conferences and congresses abroad and to keep alive more than an inner circle of the faithful in Germany itself. In fact, it was even allowed to participate in parliamentary elections. During the first World War important leaders of the labor movement, exiled because of their opposition to the war, kept in regular contact from abroad with the anti-war section of the movement that had been forced underground. Its left wing was able to participate in international meetings like the famous Zimmerwald Conference in Switzerland. Contact with the movement at home and with international brother movements made the earlier emigrations intellectually and politically more productive. The emigrants of this era are treated in a friendly way as a group of refugees. But in the Western countries they are not recognized as a political emigration. In the first years of Hitler's rule sections abroad of the German labor movement attempted on their own to keep contact with the country through frontier offices, border secretaries, and foreign literature. Elaborate headquarters flourished in Prague, Paris, Brussels, Copenhagen and Oslo. Gradually, however, persecution and the expansion of Nazism almost completely destroyed their weak organizations. By 1942 just about all of the inland contacts had been broken. Allied governments did not have the slightest un-

derstanding of the need to give the political emigrants facilities to keep up liaison with the underground. A large proportion of the emigration
abroad often felt that it was no longer bound to
the movement from which it sprang. Since Italy's
defeat and possibly spurred on by the setting up
of the Free Germany Committee in Moscow, a certain recognition of the role of political emigrants
has developed. But this change comes very slowly
and very late.

It can, however, be expected that the collapse
of the Nazi regime and the hunger of the broad
masses for freedom will awaken memories, recall
the traditions of the old movement and release
new democratic tendencies. Surviving active members of the pre-Hitler labor movement, of the religious youth movements, young intellectuals and
old democratic dignitaries will emerge as the
Nazis go down. From the underground movement, from the prisons and from the emigration
will come reliable and sincere people. Their
authority will be limited because they will have
no organization and there will be no stable democratic bodies in which to participate. It will be
hard for them to adjust to the new conditions and
to assume immediate leadership. The strength of
this leadership is bound to fall far short of the
gigantic tasks that will face it.

Thus, the anti-Nazi revolution, whatever its
opening steps may be, will begin as a leaderless
revolution. There may be "leaders" imposed from

outside—puppet leaders in the sense of Badoglio. They will have foreign, not popular authority. The picture may be confused by the fact that some popular support may be gained for the volunteer services of communists in allegiance to Moscow. But only as democratic organs develop and self-government is put into effect, can leaders prove that they are able to win independent influence by their own authority. Only then can new leaders gain experience and achieve the necessary authority for their tasks in the revolutionary democracy, by testing their influence among free people. But since a decisive role will be played at the beginning of the anti-Nazi revolution by foreign intervention, it is essential to try to understand how it might work.

III. Intervention on German Soil

TOTAL Nazi party rule ended in total Nazi war. The total Nazi war will end in the total German defeat and in foreign intervention on German soil.

Germany will pay for Hitler's war by material and moral losses unprecedented in history. But the heaviest price she will pay, will be a new delay of her own maturing, a new delay in the fulfillment of the German democratic revolution. She will be under foreign control for a long time, she will have lost her rank in the family of nations. She will live for a time with reduced sovereignty. So much she will pay for the Hitler adventure. This is the one certain point in an otherwise uncertain future. What the victorious nations are going to decide about Germany after Hitler's defeat is still an open question. In fact there has been no unity among them on the question. Two conceptions of what is to be done with Germany have been suggested. On the surface they seem as contradictory as fire and water. A "free" Germany, "stronger than the Weimar Republic" is presented as a solution by one side. A dismem-

73

bered, indefinitely occupied Germany, governed
by foreign powers, without self-government, was
advanced by the other. Of course there have been
no official commitments to either conception. But
it seems it will be difficult to reach a compromise,
even though the contradictory plans have never
received official seals of approval. They were in
the making, the power behind the facade of the
Moscow Free Germany Committee and the latter
in preparations for an AMG for Germany. However, there are important reasons and motives for
a final compromise and when the plans are more
carefully analyzed they do not appear so completely irreconcilable in view of modifications that
may easily take place on both sides.

The differences have come into the open with
the approach of victory. Once upon a time, when
no immediate victory was in sight and the threat
of defeat faced the anti-Axis powers, the first general outline of Allied war aims was formulated in
the Atlantic Charter. The Charter carries Russia's
signature, added to it by the Russian Ambassador
to Washington, Mr. Maxim Litvinoff, at a time
when securing lend-lease help was a matter of life
or death for the U.S.S.R. Nobody stuck to the
Atlantic Charter. It wandered into oblivion.
Churchill, the first day he was back home from the
meeting with the American President, gave it an
official British interpretation which denied to Germany the self-government which the Charter had
promised to victors and vanquished alike. Later,

in the United States too, the Charter became an abstraction and the "American Plan" was formulated and initial preparations made to put it in force. Finally, the U.S.S.R.'s action in withdrawing Litvinoff and sponsoring the Prussian generals in the Moscow Free Germany Committee, indicated that it did not feel bound by Litvinoff's commitment.

In reality, both the Western Allies and Russia had left the common ground on which they temporarily had been united through the principles of the Charter, with one side all out for an AMG regime, and the other dangling the seductive idea of a conservative revolution before the nose of the German army.

"This time we shall march to Berlin," both Washington and London declared, "and stay there." They prepared not only for the invasion of Germany, but for long-term occupation, for a long-lasting, international military government after the defeat and for Allied re-education of the German people. They also were unofficially committed to a policy of forestalling a revolution in Germany. Most of their plans considered the German people, including those who were consciously democratic, as passive objects. At the height of the zeal for long-term occupation of Germany, explanations and interpretations of government plans were published. Kingsbury Smith, a Washington journalist, was the author of an article published in the *American Mercury* which the editors claimed was a description of the "official" American plan for Germany. This plan not only envisaged a long-term occupation of the country, but also the economic and political dismemberment of the country and, especially, the prevention of a revolution following Hitler's defeat. The soldiers were not to be demobilized too quickly, in order to avoid revolutionary unrest. Only enough food and help should be given to keep the starving masses this side of revolution. The one thing, Smith stated impressively and distinctly, that must be prevented was revolution in Germany. The article evoked a storm of discussion and some popular protest; it was given wide circulation through the *Readers' Digest,* but government authorities never denied its official character. It was generally conceded to be a trial balloon representing views held in high and influential official circles.

On the other side the Stalin government never publicly committed itself even to invasion or occupation of Germany. Former Ambassador Grew brought home an interesting story in this connection that has never been confirmed. He told that a copy of *Pravda* reached Tokyo reporting a speech of Stalin's, which contained the promise "we shall march to the Rhine." Allegedly the entire edition was suppressed and this statement withdrawn before it became known to diplomats or correspondents in Moscow. There was Stalin's famous order of the day to the Red Army on February 23, 1943: "It would be ridiculous to identify Hitler's clique with the German people. History teaches that Hitlers come and go. But the German people and the German state remain." It is true that Litvinoff and Maisky made personal statements in agreement with dismemberment and disarmament following the "Western line," even strongly advocating it. Then Maisky and Litvinoff were withdrawn. Further, the spotlight of official Russian propaganda has been turned on the Free Germany Committee. The committee issued a manifesto urging the German people to revolt and promising as the reward for the overthrow of Hitler, redemption, self-government, a "strong" democracy—by implication—even the concession of keeping their armed forces after their retreat from conquered territories.

The conflict between these two policies has been the topic of endless discussions and treatises. It is not the intention of the author to add another. There exists a paradoxical situation. According to the best sources available, the majority of Americans and British are more in favor of the democratic principle which finds expression in the official Russian policy in regard to Germany and probably on the other hand, a majority of the deeply wounded Russian people, who have suffered more than the Western world through the German aggression, are more in favor of the principle behind the "hard-peace" policy of the Western governments. According to a report of the National Opinion Research Center in Denver, a majority of Americans believe that a distinction must be made between the Nazi government and Nazi rulers and the German people, and advocate giving a fair chance to the German people after the war. In England, the powerful Trades Union Congress voted down by an overwhelming majority a resolution condemning the German people as well as the Nazi party organization for Germany's war crimes. Moreover, an amendment favoring long-term occupation was cut out of another resolution adopted by the Congress, thus reversing the resolution adopted by the British Labour Party Conference earlier in the summer.*

There are certainly numerous British liberals and liberal conservatives who share the same opinion. On the other hand, in Russia, according to statements of Soviet writers and reports from foreign correspondents there is the bitterest hatred against the Germans as a whole. It has even found official expression. A member of the Executive Committee of the Russian Communist party, E. Z. Manuilski, in addressing the Red Army on September 29, 1943, said that the people of the Soviet Union were holding the "whole of the German fascist army" responsible for "shameful and criminal acts," setting fire to Russian towns and driving "Soviet people into German captivity. . . . Let no one say these acts of violence are perpetrated by Gestapo men, S.S., Elite Guard, and

* *News Bulletin*, O.W.I., September 14, 1943.

special detachments, by assassins and incendaries,"
Manuilski continued, "we know that power is in
the hands of German generals and that arms are in
the hands of German soldiers. They could have
stopped these crimes at any moment but they continue to execute the orders of their mad Fuehrer.
Therefore with full reason the peoples of the
Soviet Union and Red Army make the whole of
the German fascist army responsible for these
shameful and criminal acts."

Sooner or later, the position of the Western
governments will be corrected, simply by the
weight of popular opinion in their countries. A
stronger motive will be the urge for Allied unity,
the overwhelming Allied interest in a compromise
on the eve of victory. And the principles of the
Atlantic Charter, having faded out during a two
year period, may be heard again in the United
Nations. The return will not be so difficult in the
United States. Voices are already audible that an-
nounce a trend toward reversing the text and
spirit of that temporary deviation from an en-
lightened policy based on good American interests, the "American plan," described by Mr. Kingsbury Smith. In a brilliant column in the New
York *Herald Tribune* of October 5, 1943, Mr.
Walter Lippmann raised the question: Shall we
govern Germany during the occupation period?
"If we occupy and govern it will not be long before the Germans and indeed people everywhere
will begin to hold us, us rather than Germany, ac-

countable for the trouble which Germany will be in. They will forget Hitler and the military defeat." He also rejects the "Free Germany" puppet solution: "If we occupy and then govern through a free German republic the free Germans will be our puppets; as puppets they will be tainted because they will not easily make Germany prosperous and happy, they will be discredited. Worst of all, we shall merely postpone without solving them, the questions of how the Germans are going to learn to govern themselves decently. Is it not better to make the Germans face the German problem at once in its severest and most direct form, instead of giving them the shelter and protection of an Allied occupation and a military government? . . . Does anyone think the Nazi regime can be liquidated, not merely temporarily driven underground, unless the Germans themselves liquidate it? As for chaos, certainly there are good Germans. But will they ever be good enough Germans until they have done what every free people has done until they themselves have won their liberties? We can prevent the Germans from destroying our liberties, but German liberty must be won by Germans. A military government merely evades and postpones the issue." A few days before the Moscow Conference Lippmann's were the strongest words spoken in favor of a complete reorientation of previous Western plans. Moreover, they were spoken from the point of view of American interests by a man who could not be accused of being a pro-German, an outstanding defender of a strong conservative policy for America. It is the first time that a certain simple truth has been clearly formulated, namely, that there is an identity of interests between the war aims of the United Nations and a democratic revolution in Germany. This is a ray of light in the darkness, which well may point toward the direction in which the bridge over the precipice lies.

There are, of course, earlier commitments that will have to be sacrificed in order to arrive at a compromise.

In the West this would not be the first readjustment because so far the war has not even been conducted as an anti-fascist war. Lord Vansittart's ideas, for example, would have to be dropped. Certain conservative ideas that have been prevalent in the West would have to be dropped, like the policies initiated with Otto von Hapsburg, with Darlan, with the House of Savoy—the whole policy which envisaged the creation of numerous buffer states and the replacing of Nazism and fascism by clerical-fascism. Indeed most of these plans have already been discarded. But most of the long-term AMG idea would have to be dropped also.

On the other hand, Russia would have to revise the policy of the Free Germany Committee. Strong as the U.S.S.R. is now, it would reject the establishment of Western control of Central Europe. But it might drop its own special plan of

1939

Appeal of German communist leader Ulbricht from Moscow to German people:

". . . English imperialism again demonstrated its reactionary essence when it declined the proposal of Germany, supported by the Soviet Union, for the ending of the war. The national oppression in so-called Greater Germany is only grist for the mill of English imperialism, which seeks to hide its true war aims under this slogan of

1942

Appeal of German Communist party to German people from Moscow:

". . . Men and Women Workers of Germany! Rise in revolt against the Hitlerite gang of murderers. . . . Refuse to pay war taxes! Protest against compulsory deductions to meet the requirements of the war of invasion! *Set up underground Factory Committees for directing the w a r against war and Hitlerism* for a Free Germany! Get

1943

A.

Free Germany Manifesto, Moscow, July 21:

". . . the hour of collapse is approaching . . . but Germany must not die! . . . nobody will conclude peace with Hitler. . . . Hence, the formation of a genuine, national German government is the most urgent task of our people . . . *there are forces in the Army that are loyal to the country and the people and they must play a decisive role.*"

B.

Statement of Major Herbert

liberation of the Austrian and Czech people . . ."

ready for *mass strikes and demonstrations* to put an end to war and to Hitler!"

Soesslein, leading member of Free Germany Committee:

"We are opposed to fomenting demoralization in the *Wehrmacht*. We do not intend to incite the soldiers to abandon their arms and retreat in disorder. . . . We must avert at all costs any repetition of the events of 1918. We must avoid all anarchy and undisciplined behavior . . . Our slogan is reconstruction, not destruction."

making Germany its vassal, a buffer state directed
by Junker relics. A change in policy should not be
too difficult. Going back only a few years, the record shows that the current grandson of Bismarck
"line" is only one of several interpretations of the
Russian policy towards Hitler Germany. Nothing
shows that better than a comparison of communist
documents dealing with Germany for the years
1939, 1942 and 1943 (see pages 82-83).

These statements were written in Moscow by a
group of German communists, who were used as
the mouthpiece for the changing interpretations.
In 1939, they used strong words against English
imperialism and against "national oppression" in
"Greater Germany." In 1942 they begged German
workers to rise against Hitler, to set up underground factory committees to direct the war
against Hitlerism for a free Germany; they asked
for strikes and demonstrations for this purpose.
In the manifesto of 1943 they appealed to the German people and to groups in the German army to
overthrow Hitler. Subsequent statements appealed even more clearly to German soldiers for
disciplined behavior toward their officers. One aim
has been consistent: to press the fight against Hitler. Tactics, and interpretations, changed from an
appeal for a National Socialist opposition (1939)
to an appeal for a workers' revolution (1942) back
to an appeal for a conservative revolution based on
an army revolt (1943).

Increasingly conservative, rather reactionary

notes have appeared in the speeches from the Free
Germany radio desk in the Soviet capital. It took
on a more sinister note after the generals and the
high officers captured in the butchery of Stalingrad were allowed to organize a union and to enter
the Committee, their representative assuming its
Vice-Chairmanship. On October 9 a manifesto was
issued, appealing to the most reactionary of the
German Student Corps, the *Burschenschaften*, in
the archaic language of the puerile nationalist
youth cliques of the German universities of the
pre-Hitler period. On October 23 a certain
Lieutenant Colonel Boett, representing himself
proudly as an old "Steel-Helmet" man, spoke.
The Steel Helmet was the patriotic monarchist
bodyguard of the very reactionary *Deutsche Na-
tionale* Party. Colonel Boett exhorted: "Hitler
must be caused to retire and that is what I urge
you men, you who once got together in an un-
selfish way against the party politicians for law
and order. Wake up old Steel-Helmet spirit . . ."
It is nice to know that some remnants of the Harzburg Front and some of Hitler's officers and S.S.
men have turned anti-Nazi in Russia, but it is
grotesque to think of them in terms of future
liberators. Their "loyalty" to the country is
known. It is exactly the same loyalty which the
Lavals, the Francos, the Badoglios have shown; no
doubt these men want to jump on every bandwagon. They were ready to fight with Hitler yes-

terday and they are ready to fight against Hitler today, if it keeps them in power.

An odd experience, this post-mortem revival of the Harzburg Front in Moscow. What is the explanation? Is it simply a propaganda device of Moscow to demoralize the German army by using their own archaic symbols and their own old saints against the swastika and Hitler? Or is this simply a manifestation of a policy that the U.S.S.R. keeps in reserve to use in case it does not achieve a compromise with the United States and England?

Since the Moscow Conference, the Free Germany Committee has been withdrawn from the front line of propaganda into a reserve position. There it will be kept on ice until a definite compromise is reached.

Difficult as it will be to arrive at a permanent Allied compromise, it is nevertheless the only alternative to breaking the United Nations up into two separate power groups. Such a rift would endanger both groups. It would give a last chance to the beaten Nazis to maneuver out of a hopeless situation and it would enormously strengthen the position of Japanese imperialism in the East. That cannot be in the interests of any of the United Nations. It would certainly not be in the interests of the people of the Axis countries because it would restabilize the already shaken or weakened fascist tyrannies. Sometimes in history, there is no choice between a perfect solution and a less perfect one. The people of Germany have no immediate choice between freedom and tyranny, they have only a choice between foreign intervention on their soil, or the indefinite stabilization of their tyrannies. It is the price to be paid by them for the destruction of the Hitler regime. What the final accounting may be will become clearer if the various forms that foreign intervention may take are discussed. The Moscow Conference, devoted primarily to the problem of military strategy, to the problem of the second front, has hardly touched the fringes of this problem. It is still of the greatest importance to analyze the forces behind the chance of a lasting compromise in the making.

A POSSIBLE ANGLO-AMERICAN-RUSSIAN COMPROMISE

The intervention will be a product of the strength relations among the great Allied powers. Joint intervention will be the result of their compromise. The strongest power is the United States and as the war goes on its specific weight in the coalition will continue to increase. But it should not be overlooked that it is not superior in every theater of the war. The United States is the strongest world power, but the Soviet Union has become the strongest European power. The United States is engaged in a war on two fronts. The Soviet

Union has strong forces tied up in the East, but it has not shown any intention to be involved actively in the Pacific theater of war. This was confirmed by Mr. Browder, who only recently called the mere discussion of Soviet help in entering the Far Eastern war "harmful nonsense." America's war potential in Europe is further diminished by distance and transportation difficulties. One hundred million tons of steel production in the United States will mean only a few million tons of American steel on the European front at the time when the final crisis of German Nazism has started. Nor is the United States a land power like the Soviet Union. Its greatest strength is on the sea and its air force is increasing rapidly, but the fact that America entered the war late has meant that its land forces are still only a fraction of the Russian. At the present rate of organizing and providing modern equipment for newly set up divisions, it would still take many years before the United States could put a force comparable to the Russian army on the battlefields of Europe.

The same is true for the British Empire. Its production potential is much weaker than that of the United States and a large part of its army is kept on other continents, particularly in India. Its army, qualitatively, is now at least as good as the German, but Great Britain is less able even than the United States to mobilize the total number of troops needed to win the battle of Europe. In estimating the relative strength of the great powers for the intervention in Germany, potentials available in Europe and not total potentials have to be compared. At the time when the final crisis for Germany has started there are about 350 Russian divisions and a total of 170 English and American divisions in the field. In Europe itself, the proportions are much more in favor of the U.S.S.R. Although such figures supply only a rough and superficial estimate—they do not take into account the effect of naval power, air forces, military experience, etc.—they nevertheless give some basis for judging the relative strength of the powers. More important, however, is the relative political strength of the three powers in Europe. There is certainly a far-reaching English-American solidarity and cooperation. There are even groups convinced of the necessity and the possibility of a closer British-American alliance. But it is a mistake to assume that in European questions Russia is on one side, with America and Britain in complete agreement on the other. England, dependent as she is on the United States and the U.S.S.R. can by no means commit herself to joint intervention with the United States independent of Russian demands and interests. That gives Russia great additional political weight on the European continent.

From the political as well as the military standpoint, therefore, the influence of the U.S.S.R. in European questions must be reckoned to be, if not dominant, at least decisive. The achievements of

the war up till now would not have been possible
without the cooperation of all the three great
powers. Even the Russians admit that finally. But
it is certainly true that it was primarily the Red
Army that drove Germany on to the defensive,
a fact that has tremendously increased Russian
prestige. The U.S.S.R. has important political
auxiliary forces not only in eastern but also in central and western Europe. The conflicts of several
governments-in-exile with the Russian government should not mislead us as to the real influence
of the U.S.S.R. Broad groups of people in Slavic
countries of eastern Europe look upon the Soviet
Union as their liberator from Hitler rather than
as a threat to their future national independence.
It is no secret that the Western Powers have lost
the prestige which they could have had in Europe
by some of their past alliances that have not yet
been completely given up. The compromise agreement in Europe, therefore, will be a compromise
in favor of Russia or there will be no compromise
at all.

There is no doubt of the enormous strength of
Russian bargaining power. Russia's position is
strong as regards her demands for strategic frontiers, for security against a repetition of the German attack in Central Europe and for guarantees
of reparations. Concerning the Russian frontiers,
before the Moscow Conference Pravda wrote ". . .
everyone must know that the Soviet Union's
borders can no more be a topic of discussion than,

for example, the borders of the United States or the status of California." * The reference was, of course, to the Baltic States. The Russian demands will be discussed here only so far as they affect the future of Germany directly. To assure strategic borders for the Soviet Union means the re-establishment of former Russian territories in Finland, at least up to the line designated by the peace treaty concluded in 1940. In Poland the U.S.S.R. has constantly insisted on the so-called Curzon line. As late as June 19, 1943, the Union of Polish Patriots in Moscow broadcast a program which has at least as much official approval as the Free Germany manifesto. There is no indication that this program has been altered since. Some of the points pledged by the Polish patriots were: "(1) To organize the fight of the Poles together with the Red Army against the Germans . . . ; (7) To restore Polish nationality in Silesia and to re-unite [it] with Poland . . . ; (8) To return the mouth of the Vistula [Danzig] to Poland; (9) To make East Prussia Poland's outlet to the Baltic; (10) [For post-war Poland] . . . not to demand a single inch of Ukrainian, White Russian, or Lithuanian soil."

Further to the south, there has never been the slightest doubt that the Russians would demand the return of Bessarabia to the Soviet Union. The U.S.S.R. will also claim a part of the Balkans as its sphere of influence, and it will demand participa-

* *New York Times*, October 12, 1943.

tion in the control of the Dardanelles. Russian demands for strategic borders affect the future of Germany directly through the indemnity offered Poland in the form of certain districts of Germany proper, including Silesia and East Prussia.

What about the second problem, the problem of security against the repetition of German attacks? Lenin's Russia of 1917 wanted a revolutionary alliance with a revolutionary Germany. Disappointment over the failure of the German revolution to come off—a failure which the Bolsheviks ascribed almost entirely to the failure of democratic socialism in Germany—and then Hitler's attack on the U.S.S.R. has concretely remodeled the Russian conception. Is it hard to understand that the Russian people now want Germany held down so that the Soviet Union cannot be attacked a second time until she has indeed become invincible after ten or twenty years of reconstruction? They do not want any other strong power on the continent, but they certainly do not want a strong Germany, and not necessarily a communist Germany. The victorious Soviet Union rejecting the extension of the power of the Western Nations into Germany, will nevertheless not give a German democracy the chance that Lenin's Russia would have given to the Weimar Republic. It should be remembered that although certain traditions of the Lenin period are still alive the Russian regime has since been transformed. A new generation is in power, the membership of the

party has been changed both in class composition
and in function. It is different from the party of
1917. Today it is the party of the young Soviet intelligentsia to whom Soviet patriotic objectives are
much dearer than the dreams of a socialist world
revolution. For years before the war, the
U.S.S.R.'s foreign policy was concerned primarily
with the maintenance of security in order to build
socialism within the country. Even the pact with
the Nazis appeared as a permissible maneuver to
this end. The Soviet Union is not primarily interested in world revolution, but in beating down
aggressors, and in Russian reconstruction. It may
well be that it is only as a weapon to force Allied
guarantees for a joint policy in Central Europe
that she keeps the Free Germany Committee, a
kind of extra iron in the fire. As the strongest and
the most influential European power she will not
agree to less than joint control of Central Europe
and she will ask for proportionate share in this
joint control. Genuine democratic movements in
Germany would not be trusted, but they might be
tolerated on the basis of a compromise with the
Allies.

Mr. Walter Lippmann makes a proposal suggesting that the Allies should fix the German
frontiers later in the armistice period; that they
should enter Germany briefly for the purpose of
disarming her, of arresting the criminals, of recovering the loot and of making a visible reality
of her defeat. Having accomplished these essen-

tial tasks they should then "retire outside the frontiers, except perhaps to hold a strategic gateway and certain strategic economic resources such as the Ruhr and Silesia." Mr. Lippmann goes on to define this intervention by saying, "in addition, *standing outside German territory we could take under control all means of communication between Germany and the outside world*—her exports and imports and her internal finances, the ingress and egress of Germans, the censorship of mails, telegraph and radio, the movement of ships, railways and highway transport, thus Germany's foreign relations would be under Allied control." (Italics mine. P.H.) Lippmann's proposal is not so far from another that President Roosevelt included in his September, 1943, Message to Congress, when he stated, "There is one thing I want to make perfectly clear: When Hitler and the Nazis go out, the Prussian military clique must go with them. The war-breeding gangs of militarists must be rooted out of Germany—and out of Japan —if we are to have any real assurance of future peace." It is apparent that the West is prepared to offer to Russia a new basis for security in Central Europe. This may be acceptable to the Soviet Union if a concession is made in the third demand concerning Germany, which has already been semi-officially stated in Moscow.

The third demand is for reparations. In England and in America, after the experience of the last war, reparations have hardly been discussed publicly. But they play a great role in inner Russian discussion. In Russian villages tablets have been set up itemizing in rubles and kopecks the war damages that will have to be repaid. The French phrase of 1917, *le Boche payera* appears now in the Russian formula, "We shall go to Germany and fetch the industrial machines." In semi-official language it was expressed concretely by Professor Eugene Varga, noted international economic authority, in his statement from Moscow that the U.S.S.R. had a right to demand the labor of ten million German workers for ten years after the war to compensate for the gigantic destruction Russia has suffered in the war through Germany.

Assuming a readiness on the part of the Western Allies to guarantee extensive reconstruction help to the Soviet Union to grant Russia priority in German reparations, it should not be impossible to achieve a compromise here.

Anyway, in view of Russia's strength, her bargaining power, and her role in the continuation of the war in the Pacific, the Western Allies will go a long way in agreeing to Russian claims. There are important political forces in England and in America which have decided to come to this agreement. England and America both need the Soviet Union to finish the Hitler war. They both need the Soviet Union to prevent the return of German aggression. In Europe, England needs the Soviet Union and there is no serious conflict in their interests on the continent. Eastern and Central

Europe are less vital for Great Britain than are the English Channel, the Mediterranean, and Scandinavia. The defense of India is more important for the Empire than England's influence on the eastern bank of the Rhine. The Anglo-Russian agreement has a stable base and no fundamental change in its status is to be expected.

The United States is in a different position but, just as England needs Russia in Europe, the United States will be dependent on Russia's friendly neutrality in the Pacific war. The United States has no immediate and decisive interests in Europe itself. Its interests, as stated above, as the center of a broadening sphere of influence and capital expansion, are in the Western Hemisphere and in the Pacific. In spite of large American loans to Germany, the chief American capital expansion after the last war was in Central and South America, with the beginnings of larger investments in the Far East. Of course, there are American capital interests in Europe, but the most important are in Great Britain. They are larger than the trust agreements with the German chemical and machine industries. The United States will not have at its disposal an organization for world domination as strong as would be necessary to subscribe completely to plans advocated by the pure imperialists. Strong democratic forces would oppose such a policy in any case. Not all of America's vast interests can be defended equally strongly at the same time. There is no great mass inclination in

America permanently to police Europe and Germany and certainly not to police them in conflict with the Soviet Union. Once it has become clear that it is not the U.S.S.R.'s aim to Bolshevize Germany, there will be a growing tendency to concede to Russia's demands in Central Europe. The United States is too strong to capitulate but not strong enough to put up any stubborn resistance against Russia's demands. The Russian government's reconciliatory arrangements with religious organizations and churches have made it easier for conservative Americans to envisage permanent friendly relations with the Soviets.

After examination of these factors we come to two conclusions important for this essay. First, in spite of conflicts, there are no unsurmountable difficulties in the way of a final compromise. Second, a compromise will have to approximate to the Russian demands. All three major powers may find it suitable to reduce their original plans of long-term occupation of Germany, military government and complete denial of self-government. They may reach an agreement on some type of joint international control of Germany after temporary occupation, and the restitution of democratic forces with limited sovereignty. Half a year ago it seemed that dismemberment and long-term occupation might be Germany's destiny after the war. Although the conflict of interests between the presumptive victorious powers rules this out, it will still be foreign intervention in a different form which will shape the immediate future of Germany and shackle its anti-Nazi revolution. This is what the author means when he speaks of **a** dependent revolution which will encounter **great** obstacles in seeking fulfillment.

IV. Genuine Forces for Freedom in Germany

ARE there independent democratic forces in Germany? If there are, will the defeat and its consequences as described give them a chance to develop?

The defeat in this war will be an even greater blow to the German people than the defeat of 1918. Democratic reorganization may have to start from a point even further back than the period of the democratic reforms at the end of the last century. Even fair-minded people look upon this gloomy prospect as just recompense for the destruction and the suffering which Hitler's attacks have brought on the world. But it is a mistake to rely too much on a future security based on solidarity in the power coalition which will win the war. Power coalitions are not stable. They have never been. The decisive prerequisite for future security is co-lateral security and that requires a partner in the vanquished countries. Germany was the key to the war in the Atlantic world. Reduced as she will be, she will still hold in her hands one of the keys to stable and lasting peace. Hitler's defeat will liberate forces of freedom in Germany, but the conditions under which this defeat will take place are apt to shackle those same forces. Will they nevertheless emerge, and what are their prospects?

In talking of democratic forces in Germany, it is not intended to describe groups or personalities. It is wrong to rely on the effects of individuals and specific groups today. Little is known about them and about their last underground manifestations. To the best experts the nature of these forces will be a riddle until they have come out into the open. Italy has been reassuring but Germany is not Italy. However, some consolation can be found in a more abstract preview.

SOCIAL, DEMOCRATIC, NATIONAL ENERGIES

There seem to be four forces which together will operate toward the establishment of freedom in Germany.

The *first force* stems from the energies in Germany, which are the natural expression of the vital social forces of the epoch in Europe. These energies were suppressed by the Nazis, but after their overthrow they will break through again and, in spite of repeated defeat, they will show their strength once more. It is exactly these forces which some Allied leaders have feared. But you cannot make an omelet without breaking the eggs. There can be no doubt that the fascist aggression of Hitler's war was a preventive against the emancipation of these forces. The Napoleonic wars had their origin in the conflict between the feudal ruling classes and the rising urban bourgeoisie. Backward fascist Europe of the twentieth century is the scene of the conflict between the old bourgeois rulers and the struggling laboring classes. Certainly one of the decisive motives for German aggression in the last two World Wars was the defense of traditional privileges against the encroaching labor movement. The privileged groups could not have revived their claim for world conquest as they did under Hitler if they had not first achieved victory against German labor. The victors intervening after Hitler can pose great obstacles in the way of the democratic forces. But these obstacles cannot possibly be compared with the oppressive machine of the Nazis. They cannot nullify freedom as Hitler did. The intervention, willingly or unwillingly, in re-establishing certain liberties will release these freedom forces again. They will express themselves in democratic mass movements against the privileged groups, which helped Hitler to power. These movements will be the strongest factor in the new fight for freedom. Whatever occupation or international control is imposed on Germany will have to give the new labor movement not less, but more freedom than under Hitler. That will make the reactionary forces in Germany weaker than before Hitler. Hitler was helped to power by the reactionaries, but, once in power, the Nazis developed their own new privileged caste, thus undermining the old privileged groups. This new, immensely strong ruling caste controlled all of German business and industry and its power expanded continuously within the war economy. When the Nazi state machine collapses this caste will crumble. That will not mean simply the restoration of the old power of the bourgeois society of pre-Hitler time. Both the landed aristocracy and the great industrialists have steadily lost influence. After the collapse it will be evident how much. But these old privileged groups, having opposed the completion of the democratic revolution, will, therefore, be weaker this time than they were in 1917, when they effectively prevented far-reaching democratization.

Another retarding factor in 1918 was the emotional and political dependence of the middle classes on German imperialism. Two things have happened. These classes have been weakened and the middle-class intelligentsia have started to change their minds. Large sections of the urban middle classes which were formerly the chief bulwark of the Nazi movement were destroyed economically during Hitler's rule. There are people who dispute this, insisting that the formerly independent middle-class shopkeepers and artisans have become even more influential in their new jobs as masters and foremen in industry. But there can be no doubt that the old German middle classes no longer exist as a stable reactionary factor based on their former social and economic position.

The farmers are in a different category. There were progressive movements among the peasants after the last war. If the farmers of Germany are offered a democratic form of collectivization like that practised in the Scandinavian countries, with stronger farm cooperatives and state help for modernizing backward German agriculture, they will not react in a completely negative way. They need not be the reactionary factor they were when Hitler succeeded in winning them over by frightening them with threats of compulsory collectivization as in Russia. The farmers will be hostile to bureaucratic totalitarian control after their experience with the Nazis, but they have come to take planning and government regulation as a matter of course. Since a planned transformation of the war economy into economy based on need will appear to be the only way out of the chaos, the change will be popular if it is accompanied by a partial removal of the inflexible regimentation of the Nazis. Indeed the occupation or control authorities will also have to introduce planned economy. This will, of course, coincide with Russian plans, but it will not be so strange to the Western Allies either. In both England and America, government regulation has gone much farther in the second World War than in the first. Everybody knows that some planning will be necessary

even in the United States to meet the needs of
the demobilization and reconstruction period. A
reconstruction policy for Germany cannot be envisaged, except as a democratically controlled,
planned economy. In the period after the collapse
this will be the only way to start reconstruction.
Both in aims and in methods it will be fundamentally different from Nazi autarchy. It will in
the real sense of the word be an economy of need,
and its methods will tend to be democratic, since
no intervening power would, or could, emulate
the Nazi machine of oppression.

The *second force* for democracy in Germany
will be the *general craving for personal and political liberty*. This will be the unanimous popular
reaction to the totalitarian party dictatorship that
has crashed and it will wipe out the authoritarian
ideologies. A larger proportion of the German
people, after having experienced in two decades
two wars, two defeats, and the hell of the Nazi
regime will have an understanding of the real
meaning of personal freedom and other democratic liberties. The mass of the people will do
what they can to attain a greater degree of freedom and to safeguard the freedom they have.
Strong democratic movements have emerged in
Germany's past. Temporarily they achieved influence and created strong parties. They never
gained full control of Germany but, exactly because of the experience with Hitler, it is fair to
expect that such movements will finally return

stronger, more conscious and more deeply-rooted in the masses of the people than after the last war. Among the workers the traditions of the democratic fight for emancipation are actually stronger than in many other European countries. Although the continuity of this movement has been interrupted and its leading strata destroyed, so that the problem of leadership will be acute at the beginning, nevertheless there will be broad popular support and strong impelling forces for a new democracy. Even with the minimum of liberties that will be granted during the most trying period of foreign control, the spontaneous freedom movement will be able to develop into organized forms.

A *third force* in this battle for freedom will be the patriotic sentiments of the people, the urge for self-determination—provided always that the energies are brought under democratic leadership. Again, after two lost wars patriotic sentiments will not lead primarily to reactionary nationalistic ideologies. Bitter experience will have taught even backward people that chauvinism and war do not pay. The exhaustion and the shock of the defeat will make it hard for demagogues to make chauvinistic capital out of the national defeat. Even after the last war the chauvinistic reaction by itself was not strong enough immediately to reorganize aggressive German imperialism; the strength which National Socialism drew from this source is generally overestimated. It took a combination of the pan-Germanist conspirators, the core of the

Reichswehr, of the militarists and expansionists, and the great industrialists like Thyssen, fourteen years to succeed in their preparations for secret rearmament and their more open psychological rearmament. The deep shock of the economic crisis of 1930 was necessary to bring the Nazis to power. The failure of the Nazi war will have done much to discredit chauvinism and aggressive tendencies forever. But, on the other hand, since there will be foreign control, there will be national opposition; there will be the natural longing for national self-determination. Nevertheless, without democratic leadership, national pride and patriotism will remain dangerous forces, especially if there should be a lack of understanding on the part of the victors. Keeping Germany under occupation for an indefinite period and preventing the defeated Germany from assuming responsibility, as Walter Lippmann has said so clearly, would be a certain method of driving the Nazis underground to prepare for their revival. If they are to be wiped out definitely, democratic forces will have to gain leadership and channel the patriotic energies of German citizens. In that event, patriotism will reinforce the struggle for self-determination and for the inclusion of a peaceful Germany in a European and world organization. It need not follow the pattern after the last war when patriotic national forces were misguided by chauvinist groups and turned the wheels of reaction. Patriotic forces could in the long run be an irreplaceable energy leading to the completion of the democratic process in Germany.

INTERNATIONAL ASSISTANCE

These impelling forces for freedom, which will emerge in Germany, will have support among the really advanced and clear-sighted people in the victorious countries and among the liberated countries in Europe. There will be a fourth powerful factor, a *fourth force* for freedom in the post-Hitler world: assistance from progressive international forces. There are most hopeful developments now on the underground fronts. In France, for instance, important groups, in the interests of national defense, attack Nazi invaders and French reactionary collaborationists with equal vigor. There is the encouraging message the Italian people have given after twenty years of fascist oppression. There are important progressive movements in all the smaller countries who fight heroically against the Nazi oppressor. They all have their origin in similar causes. They are similar in social character and they will be sponsors of genuine democratic forces in Germany. The heroic underground forces above all in Poland, in Czechoslovakia and in Norway, have been more tolerant than some exiled cabinet members, and more conscious of future solidarity in Europe in which Germany as well as Italy will share, and not only the United Nations of today.

Finally, there are certain changes which will diminish the destructive furor of energies created by Hitler's aggression and by the necessity of defense against it. As in 1918, there will be a cooling-off time and experience will modify the very extensive intervention plans of today, once it becomes clear that the cost of carrying them out will be too great, both materially and morally, and that the desired goals are unattainable. As has been said, the first prerequisite for successful occupation, the introduction of elementary emergency measures in order to start production again, will show that compulsion can play only a small part. A great amount of productive initiative will be needed to create even the most elementary basis for reconstruction. In the long run many millions of people can be kept productive and capable of working only if their own interests are represented in the new system, only if they themselves bear a part of the responsibility and are granted a share in the future. If the defeated people offered widespread passive resistance international administrators would need immense quantities of men and materials to maintain controls and keep things going. Any successful reconstruction program, in either a liberated or conquered country, can best be launched by freeing the productive forces and those who have creative initiative. Some intervention plans have ignored this simple truth. Perhaps they will be corrected by experience.

All of these forces together create what might be called the impelling drive for the development of a democratic society in Germany. It is illusory to expect a perfect revolutionary democracy to spring out of Hitler's prison. It is safe to assume that the forces enumerated will be strong enough eventually to achieve the first steps in a new and better world. They will certainly be strong enough to bring democratic movements and parties in Germany into being and influence the international government in Germany, no matter how stubborn it may be at the start, to tolerate a mounting degree of self-government. Nobody can predict whether these forces will be strong enough to emerge as a decisive factor in the first period after the collapse or whether their struggle for recognition will extend over a long period. The time needed to create a democratic society fully conscious of its task and its aims will, in a large measure, determine the length of this struggle for recognition and equal sovereignty with the other nations in the post-war world. The corollary is also true: the nature of the foreign control will determine how effectively and how soon a democratic German society can be put into working order.

FAVORABLE AND UNFAVORABLE CHANCES

Let us keep in mind these forces for freedom: Force No. 1, the social energies; Force No. 2, the craving for personal and political liberty; Force No. 3, patriotic sentiments, energies for national self-determination; Force No. 4, progressive international assistance.

Let us make an attempt to foresee which of the possible variations of foreign intervention will set free these forces in the maximum degree of strength. This is the only way to take into account the innumerable unknowns, e.g. future developments in the war, the nature of the military decisions, the relative strength of advanced and reactionary forces within Germany itself after it is liberated from Hitler—all factors that will codetermine further development. No one can predict it in detail, but it is possible to picture what will probably happen, assuming a given variation of intervention. Of course, only some of the most important possible variations can be considered.

The variant most favorable to democratic development in Germany is at the same time the one most unlikely to occur. It could be realized only if the following conditions should coincide: Hitler has been overthrown by a revolution before final military defeat; progressive forces have steadily grown in influence in Allied countries; as a result of this and of the revolution which has helped to restore the dignity of the German people, the hatred of Germany caused by the war has partly been dissipated; the democratic forces in Germany have been able to reorganize quickly as a new *avant garde* of the nation; they have strong support for a federated Europe in a world league in which Germany is accepted as an equal; planned reconstruction is beginning with uninhibited energy. Even under such circumstances it would be impossible quickly to overcome the destruction and the exhaustion caused by the war. Nevertheless, in a comparatively short time the democratic revolution in Germany would be successfully completed and the nation would gradually recover from the setbacks of the lost war.

Such an assumption is obvioulsy taken from the world of dreams. Even the most cursory examination of present trends is enough to show there is no likelihood that the war will end in this way. A genuine revolution before the defeat is not likely, nor an intervention directed only by progressive forces, nor will hatred have vanished when Hitler breaks, nor will there be speedy renewal of democratic self-government. But these very assumptions make up an illusion prevalent among exiled anti-fascist Germans and among some well-meaning Western liberals, including Americans. It is one of the purposes of this essay to explode this illusion and to come down to the more realistic world.

Only a short while ago it seemed much more likely that quite the opposite, the most unfavorable of the possible variants was on the way, namely, that not only would reactionary and imperialist tendencies succeed in dominating the Allied countries, but that the German democratic opposition would prove weaker than expected and progressive forces would grow steadily weaker in the United Nations. In this case the reactionary forces in Germany would receive new strength even after Hitler's defeat, and no chances for a democratic rise would exist. Of course, even then the destruction of Hitler, the end of the war and the introduction of certain liberties would still mean a step forward in comparison with the world today.

The real solution may lie somewhere between the dream and the nightmare. As inner German development after the defeat will so largely be determined by the character of the intervention, let us sketch briefly the anticipated effects of the more probable forms of the coming foreign intervention.

Let us first consider Russian influence predominant in the coming intervention in Germany. In this case, some part of Force No. 1 would be set free. Even if the Soviet Union does not intend to set up a communist Germany following the pattern of its own history and experience, she has stated her intention of removing the remnants of the old bourgeois ruling classes in Germany as an obstacle to lasting peace. Whether she would work through direct occupation or with the help of a "Russian party" in Germany, like the Free Germany Committee transplanted to Berlin, is immaterial. In this event, the German people would get rid of their privileged groups, but they would pay by foreign control which at the outset would hardly permit democratic liberties and independent political parties. Force No. 2, the craving for liberty, and Force No. 3, patriotic sentiments, would play no role. Germany's development would be directed according to Russian interests. That would not liberate too much of Force No. 4, progressive international assistance. Even such a solution would be preferable to Hitler's rule. After the lapse of some time, and with the possible growth of democracy within the Soviet Union, a more independent development would be conceivable in Germany, but not during the first period after the war. The removal of the old bourgeois ruling classes would be paid for by a regime in which no German Alter or Erlich could live in freedom. Therefore, a solution involving strong one-sided dependence would hardly find much support among the greater part of Germany's people. And that would weaken the stability of the peace and darken the outlook for the world. (The German people's present inclination to surrender to the East is, therefore, probably overestimated.)

The second possibility is the "Western variant." This would come if the influence of the Soviet Union were largely eliminated and the solution of the problems of Central Europe were undertaken by the bourgeois democratic countries under American leadership. Such a solution, dear to some Americans, would presuppose either that in

Western countries intransigent conservative and reactionary tendencies were dominant, or that the alliance with the Soviet Union was undermined and Russia out of the picture for military reasons. It has been shown that this variant is highly improbable in view of Russia's strength. But let us discuss it nevertheless. The intervening forces would then probably work with "moderate" Nazis or would have to support some kind of Badoglio in Germany, using them as a bulwark and as a force of "law and order." In this case, Germany's old privileged classes would take on new life and there would be the strongest resistance to the maturing of social revolutionary forces. Force No. 1, the revolutionary social energies, would certainly not be set free, since this intervention would come to Germany with the purpose of restoring the "free economy" of traditional capitalism. There would be some release of Force No. 2; vassal political parties would recruit their leadership from the remnants of the pre-Hitler bourgeois society, from certain strata of public officials, from conservative churchmen and maybe some old right-wingers among the trade unionists and party leaders of the old Social Democracy. That would be another type of Free Germany Committee, which, as Mr. Lippmann says, would also be composed of puppets—tainted puppets. There would, of course, be great resistance against freeing Force No. 1, both on the part of international authorities and on the part of reactionary German groups, their puppets. There would be, therefore, no freedom of national self-determination even if dismemberment and re-education plans were enforced less strictly than originally intended. Some freeing of Force No. 2 and very little of Forces Nos. 1, 3, and 4 would be the result of the "Western variant" of intervention. It would still be preferable to a Hitler Germany. In the long run there might be some chance of social reforms. But there is great likelihood that Germany would face the common danger of buffer states, the danger of becoming involved in a new conflict as a vassal power. The restoration of German capitalism dependent on foreign capital would serve the interests of foreign capital but neither the interests of the people of the Allied countries nor the people of Germany. This seems, by the way, the only possible form in which German capitalism could be temporarily restored, namely, as an agency of great international trusts.

Finally, the third variant is that intervention policy in Germany will be determined by a balance of Eastern and Western, Soviet and Anglo-Saxon influences. This is fortunately, as explained, the most likely form intervention will take and it needs further, closer investigation. Indeed, it would set free a maximum of Forces Nos. 1, 2, 3 and 4. There would be social reforms, there would be civil liberties, there would be more self-determination than under any other conditions, and there would be encouragement for progressive people in victorious countries to work to further it without having to be afraid of endangering their national interests.

There are several possible forms of such a joint policy. The first we shall discuss is joint occupation formerly thought of as the only possibility, and which has not yet been definitely discarded. Joint occupation may take one of two forms: division of Germany according to zones, each administered by one of the victor powers, or a mixed occupation administration.

Division into separate zones would be extremely difficult for economic reasons alone. It is not easily conceivable that production could be restored if the German economic body were divided into two or three parts, each with a different administration and with a different center of gravity. It might easily be a first step toward final dismemberment and toward the incorporation of parts of German productive forces in the diverse economic systems of the neighboring victorious countries—one part into the sphere of trust capitalism in the West, another part into the sphere of Russian state economy in the East. Joint occupation could also mean limiting the occupying forces to the maintenance of order, police control and purely administrative tasks. This kind of occupation would require extensive German collaboration. The difficulty would remain the necessity for compromise on social questions, as neither the complete application of Russian principles nor of Western methods would be possible. It is clear again from this illustration that the closer the cooperation between the Allies and the more their steps are joined, the greater are the chances for a democratic development in Germany itself. It is by no means out of the question that Soviet commissars and AMG officials could work out an occupation scheme together. Social transformations have taken place in the West as well as in the East during the war, and they have tended to bring more closely together the two types of social systems which were once so different. But great difficulties exist and the Russians are suspicious of the establishment of non-European forces on the continent in any form. Therefore, a highly possible Allied compromise would be *agreement on non-occupation of Germany.* Only a short time ago it would have appeared as wishful thinking even to conceive of such an eventuality, but now it is being taken under consideration by important Allied representatives. This kind of solution would mean short joint occupation as the last act of the war. Under the occupation Germany would be disarmed, the first emergency steps for reconstruction would be initiated and the war criminals punished. Then joint occupation would be replaced by a democratic self-government of Germany under inter-Allied controls. If there is to be foreign intervention and government, joint intervention is the least of the evils in the eyes of a German democrat, but joint non-occupation is the best of the solutions that have been considered. Even that could be worse than Versailles. Mr. Lippmann's proposal, for instance, envisages more extensive international control than there was after 1918. The author has never shared the ideas of Nazi propagandists that the Versailles Treaty was the base of all evil, but he is convinced that it did create many of the poisons which finally resulted in the Hitler sickness. Therefore, it is not only in Germany's interest (at present that counts least of all), but it is in the interests of the world that a joint solution be found and that it take the form of a joint control of a free Germany. This would not only save Germany from one-sided dependence as a vassal state on either the East or the West; it would not only avoid the breaking up of the United Nations' alliance in rival groups; but it would also bring about democratic and social reforms and it could, without endangering Germany's neighbors, bring security. This would permit the only development that would finally make Germany a strong pillar of a stable peace system, the fulfillment of Germany's democratic revolution and the regaining of her full sovereignty. If Germany becomes a protectorate of the victorious nations, its democratic movement would naturally be under the joint protection of the progressive forces among the Allies. In the best circumstances, Germany would soon join the United Nations as an equal among equals. How far back

Hitler has driven the world that only a short time ago it seemed Utopian to hope for anything approaching a real solution! Even today, writing this before the Moscow Conference, the author feels like a man who is waking up from a nightmare, not yet sure that it was only a bad dream.

It is important that this point be understood. The best possible solution that can be expected will still be only a compromise. No "protectorate" can set free the full potential of the creative forces inherent in the vanquished nations after they have gotten rid of their fascist usurpers. No true German or Italian socialist, democrat or liberal, will ever be really reconciled with the best compromise. But they will have to accept a compromise as the only starting point for a period of patient and peacefully acquired reform. The announcement of an agreement on occupational zones granting Russia East Elbia, the Western Powers West Elbia, dividing Germany into two halves, is a bad omen for the final solution! Germany, divided in two pieces, would become the seat of the greatest irredentist movement of all times.

V. The Program of a Revolutionary Democracy

NO PROGRAM has yet been formulated by German democrats. That should surprise no one who has given some thought to the conditions in Germany. The future democratic leaders within the country have lived through eleven years of tyranny. It was not just physical oppression; they were practically robbed of their freedom of thought by a system which, even among anti-Nazis, induced an acquiescence in unprecedented barbarism committed in the name of the German people. They did not dare even to confess their feelings to friends. This is hardly fertile soil for the growth of good thinking and balanced reasoning. Contrast this with the United States or England, where year after year discussions have been going on between the best minds on how to conduct the war, on peace terms, and on reconstruction. Nevertheless, when the fetters are broken and the first group of conscientious objectors against Nazism and all that it means gather together in the turmoil and chaos of total collapse, there will be many people with common sense and genuine democratic feeling and there will be millions in despair about what to do and where to go. Those who are looking for a new way of life will start with the most primitive, the most simple steps first. No system of thought, no programmatic charter could be expounded in detail in advance; there are, in addition to the shock of the birth of this movement, too many unknowns in the picture. Whichever of the variants of intervention on German soil comes to pass, the democratic objective will be to coordinate the maximum number of the moving forces behind the revolution and shape them into the first effective nucleus of a democratic society.

If there is no such thing yet as a program for German democrats, there are foundation stones in the thinking and writing of refugees abroad and, of course, more foundation stones in the surviving traditions of the former democratic movements, and still more in the active centers of underground resistance.

Within Germany the alpha and omega of underground activity wherever groups have the strength to meet, is the effort to do the utmost possible to help overthrow Hitler, to work toward the immediate ending of the war and to remove the party tyranny.

Later, other tasks will come with the unfolding of the revolution, efforts to gain recognition for self-government and self-determination, the setting up of a revolutionary provisional government. The liquidation of the heritage of the war in the broadest sense and the lasting and permanent inclusion of what is left of Germany, purged and redeemed, in the world union of United Nations are objectives that belong to a later stage.

AWAY WITH HITLER

As long as the war lasts and Hitler still controls the murderous German power machine, there can be only one immediate goal—to help break it from within, and in every way possible coordinate the scattered nuclei of the atomized anti-Hitler forces in Germany for the overthrow of the world's and Germany's arch enemy, National Socialism.

If these forces were strong, organized and influential, they would prepare for armed revolt. From outside we shall never know exactly how strong they are before they come into the open. There is some evidence, that the slow-motion growth has recently taken on a faster tempo. But the factors that limit this development have been enumerated. The "third front," the revolutionary inner front of this war, will probably not reach strength comparable to the military front or even comparable to the guerrilla fronts of the oppressed nations, until after the defeat and until intervention has already started. That has been true in Italy. But make no mistake about the potentiality of this silent front.

This front may unexpectedly be able to accelerate the final crisis of the Nazi regime in a way not directly dependent on the military situation. There may still be large armies and several hundred divisions in the field; experts may have calculated that so many divisions are needed to break them within a set time according to the most scientific military and strategic evaluations; and the inner front may strike a decisive blow before the estimated time. The general ideas, the aims and the program which the forerunners of this front have formulated in underground circles and in exile abroad will help to crystallize the new program. (Even though in the underground and among the emigration they may have had no visible success, influence or authority.) To say this does not mean to subscribe to the illusion that the German emigration, which is confused and discouraged like every emigration, which is probably more out of touch, less independent and more under the influence of political fashions in Allied countries than any previous emigration, could create a revolt of its own will or when the revolt comes, that it could give it aim and direction. The influence that the Allies could exercise through their propaganda would be a thousand times as strong, if it seemed opportune to them to foster a revolt. For instance, the Allies could change from the formula of unconditional surrender to the formula of unconditional surrender of Nazism and its allies. But even if Allied propaganda did help in the West, it would still be the task of the German anti-Nazis themselves to help in building the political and the practical foundations for the popular uprising. The Moscow Free Germany Committee has already been mentioned several times. One may reject its line, suspect its motives, sincerely regret that it involves the support of only one Allied country—for which the leaders of the U.S.S.R. probably should be blamed least, considering the color blindness in political warfare of some of her partners—but it still remains a unique model of political warfare. Used jointly by the United Nations with aims mutually agreed upon, it could be a deadly weapon against Hitler's political spine as the symptoms of political paralysis of Nazism become obvious.

Why don't the Allies in the West make use of this weapon? This is how Lord Vansittart answers: We don't need any advice on how to beat Hitler politically "for the simple reason that we are going to beat Hitler militarily." The argument for the wrong side could not be better stated. Of course, what Vansittart implies is not true, since the use of the political weapon in this war has been more extensive than in any previous war. For a time the Nazis were the masters; even now one of their last hopes is politically to move out of a desperate military situation. As a matter of fact, no one in the Allied camp really believes in Vansittart's formula, least of all himself or he would not be the leader of Vansittartism which is nothing else than political warfare. What Vansittart really meant to say was: We don't want political warfare of the kind proposed because we don't believe in an anti-Nazi potential in Germany, because we think the underground movement is, if not swindle, then fantasy and we don't like the German revolution either. And that is the explanation for the political strategy in the West which, by and large, has refrained from encouraging revolt. It has been considered ineffective and "ideological" to encourage revolution, but the propaganda actually used by England and America has been simply "ideological" for different objectives. It seems that Western prejudices against a revolution on the continent, in whose genuine democratic character no one could believe if not familiar with the real underground of Europe, played a bad trick on the Allied cause. Even worse has been the surprisingly gentle political treatment of the Nazi system by some British and American leaders, while others influential in directing political strategy, have generalized a kind of anti-Germanism. All this has not encouraged the people's revolt, it has handicapped the only partner there is behind Hitler's lines, it has undermined the elements of democratic revolutionary forces in Germany which existed all through this war. The gigantic potentials of these forces are not utilized even now. Once they are set in motion, it is likely that they will still be hindered. There are people who want the overthrow of Hitler and unconditional surrender of Germany but who are frightened by what must then follow according to the most elementary laws of history —the revolution. They hope to escape the profound changes to come. These are the same people who played ostrich several years back when Hitler had risen to power and was already threatening their lives. Do most Americans and Britishers remember that they have successful revolutions in the past to thank for their present freedom? From the teachings of their own histories they may know that there are certain periods in the lives of nations in which the only principle of legitimacy is the principle of revolt against the tyrannous usurper at home. There were many anti-Nazi Germans who have hated and fought German militarism all their lives, who were moved by the Moscow appeal for a conservative revolution. They listened to that appeal, although it inexcusably paid homage to the past glory of the Prussian sword, because it seemed to sound the first note of the call they had waited for: Revolt against Hitler, purge yourselves by throwing the tyrants out and regain your dignity, then you will be our friend and not our enemy.

But the real call has not yet come. If German anti-Nazis were able to draw up a concrete program of future action they would set down a chart of the indispensable first steps needed to get the Nazis out. The program would probably include the following rough points:

(1) The removal of the Hitler government and the arrest of all its members.

(2) The dissolution of the Nazi party and of all the other Nazi organizations, the arrest of all their leaders and sub-leaders.

(3) The removal of all commanders of the army, the call to all troops to march home, to demobilize immediately after reaching home, this to be carried out under the leadership of soldier representatives from each military unit.

(4) The dissolution of the entire S.S. and the immediate arrest of its officers, leaders and sub-leaders.

(5) The dissolution of the Nazi police, the arrest of all Nazi police officers and the immediate setting up of local safety units.

(6) The immediate election of shop stewards in the factories, mines, mills, shops, and offices on the basis of the Weimar law and the formation of factory or plant councils, the elections having been organized by reliable anti-Nazi workers (the men and women in the factories know who the reliable anti-Nazi are).

(7) The formation of popular local councils in the villages and in districts of the towns and cities.

(8) The establishment of regional provisional government committees made up of delegates from the chief factory and local councils.

(9) Immediate arrest of all higher officials of the administration, including higher municipal officials, and the provisional continuation of the

administration by mixed committees made up of lower officials who, during the time of the Hitler rule and the war, had an attitude friendly to the people and to the workers, and who are ready to maintain a provisional emergency administration under the control of local representatives of the popular councils.

(10) The arrest of all higher economic officials of the Reich and the continuation under lower officials of an emergency administration, especially in those offices responsible for planning the economy, this apparatus all to be under the control of shop stewards and other labor officials from plants and factories who will work with the popular councils.

(11) The removal and arrest of all judges and higher justice officials of the Third Reich, and the immediate setting up of popular tribunals to sentence Nazi leaders and war criminals.

(12) The immediate confiscation of all Nazi party properties, the arrest of all their directors and leaders; the arrest of all the leaders of Industry Groups, district economic advisors, trustees, and their chief assistants, the administration of all such machinery to be taken over by labor representatives.

(13) The immediate arrest of all chief functionaries of the Labor Front, the confiscation of its property, the immediate creation of local committees to re-establish the free trade unions.

(14) The arrest of the leading officials of the

Farm Estate, the Agricultural Front, the Artisans Front, and the various middle class and cultural "fronts."

(15) The immediate dissolution of the Hitler Youth, the arrest of all professional state youth leaders.

(16) The immediate suspension of the entire National Socialist press, the arrest of the editors, and a guarantee of complete freedom of the press for anti-Nazis.

(17) The immediate taking over of radio broadcasting facilities by local soldiers' and workers' delegations and the arrest of all leading Nazi propagandists.

(18) The immediate closing of all the Adolf Hitler Training Schools (the *Ordensburgen*), and the arrest of their teachers; the temporary closing of all universities and technical institutes, primary and secondary schools to be re-opened after the purging of the teaching staffs under the control of local labor and soldier delegations and representatives of cultural organizations who had demonstrated their anti-Nazism—for example, liberated political prisoners.

(19) It is self-evident that all international treaties, military alliances and practically all special laws of the Nazi era will have become null and void.

The American reader will ask whether it will be possible in the first hour to create a provisional government out of tested people, recruited from the underground movement and from among liberated prisoners, which will have authority and which will be able to win the confidence of the people. There are no democratic mass organizations in Germany, no political parties, and there is no generally recognized anti-National Socialist authority. Nevertheless, local councils and even larger regional bodies made up of delegates of local councils will be possible at once. There are enough proven and reliable anti-Nazis in every town and in every district, who will be known locally and recognized quickly enough. Just imagine that you have lived in a village or a small city for ten years under fascist rule. Would you not after that time know who is who among your neighbors? You would be able to walk through the streets of your village or your neighborhood, from house to house, and point out the window of the one who served the evil and the other who resisted it, who suffered, and perhaps even gave heroic evidence of his unbreakable convictions. It will be more difficult in large cities, where community ties are looser. But in the residential areas of big cities such ties exist, and the close association of working people in the shops, the offices and the great factories is most important. Underground reports have given information for years that the authority of the intransigent anti-Nazi increased after the first wave of Nazi infection which had stigmatized those it did not murder or imprison. Yes, the jailbird of yesterday is very often the political leader of tomorrow.

There has hardly ever been a time in which leaders have been tested, approved, honored and respected as much as those will have been who return from the terror cellars alive. For many weeks in Italy local papers, having so quickly shed their fascist editors, were full of stirring articles every day, hailing the men who had returned from Lipari, the island of the banned, from the camps and from the prisons. Future presumptive AMG officials are breaking their heads quite unnecessarily over the question of who will be able to take over local affairs. If the people are only permitted to go their way, guided by their own experience, they will prove able to master the most urgent problems. They will storm the prisons, as was done in Italy, to get out those they love and need. They will follow the men: they know them. The population, Germans, foreign conscript workers and war prisoners, clamoring for peace, freedom and bread, will certainly support any provisional local authority that seems to be trying to secure these benefits for them. There will still be a lack of experienced leadership, but the only way to develop leadership is through practice in freedom. Does anyone think that the promise of foreign education for, say fifty years, will produce responsible democratic authority? Such a promise might even break the democratic nuclei and prepare a worse nationalism than there has ever been in

Germany. Experience with the Irish and the Indians, and, most recently, with the Italians, should be warning enough. Tolerance on the part of occupying armies of the democratic forces is the very least the Allied leaders can insist upon in their own interests.

THE UNFOLDING OF DEMOCRATIC INSTITUTIONS

During the transitional period the revolutionary forces will be trying to overcome their weaknesses and to develop more mature democratic institutions, to combine local and regional groups in order to create a nationally representative authority. Factory and local councils will be adequate in the first phase; more developed democratic organizations, cooperatives, political parties, trade unions, must be organized as quickly as possible. Democratic bodies will have to develop that will transcend the local units and that will be in a position quickly to put an emergency program into effect, to carry out demobilization and to achieve recognition from the occupation authorities. The conditions that will exist when Nazi power collapses must be kept clearly in mind, in considering how deeply the spontaneous mass movements will shake the entire social structure. At the same time it must be remembered how difficult it will be, even for the best-trained occupation authorities, to master the administrative and economic machine controlling what will still be the torso of the Hitler Empire. Then it will be apparent that even those Allied leaders who shy away from revolution will have to cooperate with revolutionary organs, since their only alternative would be to cooperate with the Nazis. We know from experience that it is not impossible that after the capitulation the victors will use parts of the conquered military and police machinery. Such things have happened in history before. They were happening in Italy. However, we doubt whether any German Fouché will have a great chance of recognition. The name of the most logical person to fill the role of the French Fouché is not even Goering, it is Heinrich Himmler and you certainly cannot do business with the chief of the S.S. and Gestapo. Or perhaps after all you can. The person to play a modern Fouché must be able to "deliver." Even Badoglio, glorious fascist marshal, was not able to deliver substantial forces! (The navy? But the Italian navy, says Professor Salvemini, rightly, came on its own, quite without Badoglio; it had only the choice between coming and scuttling.) It is difficult to see how anybody in Germany could "deliver" except the chief of the special troops.

It is very likely that the dependent democratic revolution will have its chance. This is something which the enemies of the revolution do not want to concede and which most observers do not realize. That does not mean that any revolution can prevent the occupation or basically change its political character through its strength alone. But, the occupation regime can be influenced. There are factors that will make it more tolerant toward the democratic movement:

First of all, the question of self-government. Until recently the Western Allies were not planning to recognize a provisional German government. But political parties and other national units will develop inevitably from the spontaneous local representative bodies. The Allies could prevent this by forbidding any kind of political parties at all. (That indeed was tried out for a short time in Sicily, but it did not work there.) Such a ruling for a longer period would not only be contrary to all the traditions of the British and Americans, it would also increase their administrative problems in Germany to an extraordinary degree. The carrying out of the most elementary tasks is practically impossible without German cooperation. Cooperation with Germans will naturally tend to go beyond the drafting of local assistants. Even the immediate and acute problem of finding substitutes to fill a hundred thousand responsible civil service posts can hardly be solved without help from central bodies. Substitutes for this bureaucracy can be adequately supplied neither by the Allied expeditionary corps of administrative officials, nor by moderate Nazis, supported by the Allies. Finally, as a result of the necessity of taking on people from below there will have to be consultation with the national bodies of those organizations which have specialized knowledge of personnel, and can give political guarantees. These organizations will logically be the new trade unions, the cooperatives, and the newly developed or the revived political parties. This is exactly what happened in spite of elaborate AMG plans for Italy, made out on the green baize desk. What political parties may be expected in Germany? There will be some party center of democratic labor, some new Catholic popular center, and there will be communists, to mention the most important. There may be a more conservative freedom party around people like Niemoeller, supported by conservative sections of the youth, such as those who issued the Munich Manifesto. In short, again, the picture will be similar to the one in northern Italy, with the "six-party" committee. There the more important were the democratic Catholic Action party, the Liberal Socialist, the Communist, the Action party and Guistizia e Liberta.

Not for a second could it be assumed that, in a country like Germany with its tradition of organizational skill, the development of new representative organizations like these could be prevented once democratic principles and civil liberties have been reintroduced. The trend toward self-government, therefore, will insist on recognition.

In the second place, a similar problem will exist as far as immediate economic measures are concerned. The extent of the economic collapse will mean that, at least in initial stages, such restrictions as rationing, the control of labor markets, and priorities will have to be maintained. Germany's economy, after having been geared for years to the Hitler war, will be completely unable to function in the emergency if the attempt is made, as some groups among the Western Allies envisage, to return to free competition and profit economy. Germany cannot supply herself with raw materials from free markets nor can she initiate foreign trade in free international markets. She cannot live on the other side on the level of the village. To feed millions of starving workers and their families or to give them jobs will be the alternative for the victors. What kind of jobs will it be possible to create? For the duration of the war in the Far East, and as long as the occupational powers have only a part of their forces in Europe, German territory will necessarily be included in the Allied war economy, that is, in a kind of state-controlled economy. Government regulation of industry, as developed under fascism, could not suddenly be removed, even by giving bankrupt German capitalists orders for war supplies for the Allies. The more important concern of the occupation authorities will be to institute emergency measures necessary for *rebuilding devastated areas and reorganizing transportation, providing emergency housing and supplying food and clothing for starving and homeless people in view of the lack of consumers' goods of all sorts.* To carry out these emergency measures, the occupation authorities will have to rely on municipalities, on factory councils, on cooperatives, and not on the monopolists of Hitler's war economy.

Third, temporarily there will be a certain parallel between the interests of the democratic movements and of the occupational authority in regard to economic sanctions. The democratic movements will tend to abolish the privileged groups of the Nazi state. Badoglio had to start investigations of the fortunes of fascist profiteers. Even in the Mussolini territory in the north, such an investigation had to be promised. There is never a great crisis in which a request by the masses for the abolition of privileges does not appear. Who could stifle the unleashed and just demands for such purgings in the coming upheaval of millions in Germany, who have seen the riches from their labor go to the Nazi war profiteers? The occupational authorities, if only for the technical reasons mentioned, will not be able to get along without freezing large industries and other monopoly property. Occupation authorities may want to respect the interests of the privileged groups but will find it impossible, and so the temporary measures instituted will have to be in accord with the general direction in which Germany's democratic movement is going. The five hundred to a thousand leading men of Germany's big business may be able to avoid arrest by the occupation authorities, they will hardly escape strict regulation of their properties. Not only the German underprivileged will be asking for that, but also both the large and small Allies of the Western Powers, the U.S.S.R., the small nations, and the Jewish people.

The same will be true of the great estates of the Junkers, the landed aristocracy. Even conservative groups in Allied countries acknowledge the war guilt of the German military caste which has its base in the landed estates. For more than a century the democratic movement in Germany struggled vainly to break the privileged position and the virtual political hegemony of the Junkers, a total of about fifteen thousand families among a people of seventy millions. Even Hitler did not protect all of their privileges once he had gotten the backing of the Junkers for his conquest of power. The story is told in the memoirs of an old whip of the Junker group, Oldenburg Januschau, who was instrumental in convincing his friend Hindenburg of Hitler's usefulness, when the Schleicher government was threatening to cut the subsidies to the Junker estates. Januschau's book, which he wrote just before he died after some years of experience with the Nazis, is the elegy of a cheated crook. He had cheated the Kaiser's government successfully in the last war; then he cheated the Republic. Then he tried it under Hitler, with a negative result. He is only an example. Whatever survives of his class will be further weakened in the defeat. The landed aristocracy everywhere stubbornly resist modern reforms that infringe on their privileges, but they are not immortal. Americans need only remember their Civil War.

There are two outstanding pressures which will break the remnant of Junker power after Hitler. The most immediate will be the urgent need to find land at home for about a half million German nationals who were settled by Hitler in conquered territories, many of whom he brought from other former German settlements to please his allies. These people would be killed if they tried to stay on in Hitler's vanished *Lebensraum*. They have already started to return home to Germany in panic. The other pressure, which will become insistent later, is the refusal of any future government in Germany to subsidize the Junkers. If it is a foreign government it will want to export its own cheap grains to Germany. If it is a German government its interest will be in importing cheap grain, not in subsidizing the parasitic and bankrupt landed gentry of the past on their archaic and uneconomical estates. Immediately after the defeat, purely technical reasons will lead to a disregard of Junker privileges. For example, the food shortage will necessitate the confiscation of the stocks of the great estates. The old army and officers' caste will, of course, be liquidated in line with armistice or peace demands, as will the staffs of the military academies. In short, the traditional centers of power of the Junker caste will be destroyed. Thus, at least a partial removal of the old class privileges in Germany will result from the simple and inevitable emergency measures of the occupation, that same occupation which will want to avoid the German revolution. In order to reinstate the German field marshals and Junkers— Herr Schacht, the economic directors of the I.G. Farben Industrie, Messrs. Krupp and Thyssen, all of whom will "yearn for" liberty after the defeat —even the most modest liberties just granted to the people liberated from Hitler would have to be taken away again. The Nazi party machine gone, a new foreign apparatus of oppression would have to be installed. To be sure, it is not entirely impossible that events will take this course, but it is not very probable, primarily for the reason that the victorious armies will be composed not only of conservative planners, but also of tough soldiers and officers who will not have come to Germany to protect the fattest war profiteers and those who were chiefly responsible for this war. In Sicily, the best conservative intentions did not work. The plan was to take "non-active fascists" and even formerly "active fascists" into the AMG apparatus. But they did not trust this peace; they all ran away—police officials and prefects as well as the well-to-do fascist society crowd.

It will only be after the occupation has been established that the period of immense difficulties for the further course of the German democratic revolution will begin.

What the Freedom Movement Will Demand

Though at first the interests of the democratic revolution and the Allies will be parallel in some respects, once the occupation is completed a divergence of interests will become apparent, even a danger of conflict. Up to that time there will have been basic agreement in the most urgent tasks, namely, to fight the German war machine and end the war, to abolish Hitler's party regime, to set up a provisional emergency government, to avert chaos, to get production going again, and to start reconstruction.

The democratic revolution will then naturally try to defend its rights against encroachments from any side, and that includes restrictions imposed by the occupation authorities. Democratic interests will be served if the energy of the social-revolutionary forces is directed toward overcoming the breakdown and increasing production and productivity. The danger exists that, for a variety of reasons, the Allies will try to inhibit the social-revolutionary forces.

Furthermore, the democratic revolution will necessarily aim at full self-government, unlimited democratic liberties and equal status in an international order for vanquished and victor alike. It will press forward toward these goals, holding firmly to the belief that no lasting peaceful union of nations can be based on a system of privileged and underprivileged nations. However, foreign intervention, whatever form it takes, will necessarily mean some limitation placed on self-government and a kind of tutelage until a responsible German regime is recognized. Until final peace conditions are formulated the mere existence of an occupation regime will necessarily be an imposition against national self-determination.

It will depend on the peace terms how profound a conflict will develop between the German democratic forces and the Allies and how long that conflict will last. But the nature of the peace terms will depend in part on the democratic forces of Germany. True, the German democratic revolution may not be able to prevent occupation but it can modify the character of the occupation to a certain degree and exert some influence on the peace terms. The more convincing the program of the democratic revolution, the stronger will be its influence on analogous groups in the Allied camp and on the final decisions of the Allied leaders. The strength of the democratic movement will depend on how well it is able to explain its program to the liberated people of Germany and to the people of the Allied nations. It will also depend on its ability to supply adequate leadership in the form of a political party or a coalition of its most important democratic groups to challenge the dependent and parasitic groups which will inevitably try to seek protection behind the backs of the invaders. Here there is space only to sketch the chief arguments for the freedom movement as opposed to the most important of the dependent groups. We shall come back to organizational problems later.

In order to complete the social-revolutionary change the freedom movement will ask for *a system of social planning as against the restoration of a profit economy*. All of its factions will ask for that. It will be easy enough to present convincing historical arguments to support this point. Both in 1914 and in 1939 it was the economically privileged groups in Germany that drove the country into the war and played the outstanding part in the conduct of the war. People tend to forget this fact as far as the old Imperial Germany is concerned. Actually, there have been groups among the Allies and among conservative Germans who have hoped that this war would bring back the Kaiser and replace National Socialism by a conservative restoration. That was before the Kaiser refused a friendly invitation to London, answering he would like to get there only after victorious German troops! But the Allies fought the last war to put a democratic Germany in the place of the Kaiser's Germany! As the surviving heirs of the old privileged aristocracy are now so closely interrelated with the Nazi party regime—the big industrialists as well as the Junkers, the offspring

of the princes as well as of the industrial barons—
it will not be too difficult in Germany itself to
keep the relatively weak tendencies towards a conservative restoration in check. However, it is not
impossible that plans for a conservative or monarchist restoration may emerge once more in
Washington or London, though they would find a
more appropriate atmosphere in Hollywood. The
Italian King's example is illuminating.

Perhaps some conservative leaders among the
Allies will again have forgotten that Hitler prepared his war jointly with the Pan-Germanist
heroes of the Harzburg Front—the political coalition of big industrialists and militarists—and with
the Bavarian reactionaries after 1930. Even esti-
mable men, like Faulhaber and even Niemoeller,
who later became anti-Nazis, had once participated involuntarily in the preparations for Hitler's victory at home, because they were intimately
associated with these reactionary forces. Their
motives were certainly different from those of
Krupp and Thyssen. Thyssen's own published
confession is singularly candid in this regard. Perhaps these men too have learned. But no conservative restoration, modernized and moderate as it
might be, could give us the slightest security
against a third repetition of German aggression.
There are objective factors which would inevitably drive its leadership anew into competition
against, rather than cooperation with, other nations. In Germany these forces are anti-democratic

in principle. Today, now that the war is lost, some of them are discovering that they have a "Western heart." But it was the same in 1918. The representatives of heavy industry since Bismarck's time and of the chemical industry since 1918, quite naturally and with only negligible individual exceptions, have been the chief exponents of German imperialism. In Bismarck's time they submitted to the Junker regime. Later, under the Kaiser and during the Republic they shared the power with the Junkers and with them sponsored and protected the camouflaged re-militarization behind the façade of the Republic. When Hitler made his appearance they backed him. For more than a hundred years, the influence of the Junkers has been *the* German anachronism. To restore the privileges of the feudal castes and of the industrial monopolists, no matter to what degree at the outset they were dependent on foreign capitalism, would mean an artificial prolongation of an archaic Germany, and the first step towards an inevitable third aggression.

It is not only the convincing reasons based on historical experience that will make the program for democratic socialism carry weight with the starving German people. The mass unemployment during the years after the last war (which was not prevented by the flow of credits from England and the United States) has not been forgotten. Removal of caste privileges to control the means of production will be an indispensable part of the emergency planned economy after the defeat. As has already been said, the monopolies are not going to have foreign markets and there will be no markets for them in Germany. The smaller industries will be unable to open up their plants. Whether German production starts again will not be determined by the profit-seeking of privileged groups. This is true both for big industry and the large estates. Germany's agricultural production, backward for decades, has been kept going by expensive state subsidies and a system of preferential tariffs. Technical improvements and the modernization of German agriculture—one of the decisive prerequisites of German reconstruction—will require agrarian reforms and a cooperative type of collectivism. To attempt to conserve economically privileged groups after the war in Germany, or to reopen the competitive fight between them would be to pronounce a death sentence on millions of Germans, and to endanger Europe's reconstruction. The rise of productivity would immediately be curtailed. Meanwhile the danger would exist that the traditional upper classes, thus bolstered, would prepare the ground for another aggressive venture. Therefore, the social program of a freedom movement has to be *a system of democratic planning, as against a restoration of profit capitalism.*

The productive masses in Germany will understand these matters better than some of their victors. The misery of the Germany of tomorrow will hardly be imaginable for the average American, except for soldiers who will see the drama, just as they witness the tragedy of the Italian people now. But even in the West, there is a growing understanding of the inevitability of government regulation during a war and during a depression. When kindred movements in the West become aware of the difficulties of demobilization in their own countries, they will also acquire a better understanding of the necessity for an economic system in Germany directed toward public welfare and not private profit. This understanding will be increased when they are actually confronted with the devastation and the disorganization on the old continent. The thesis of the apologists for the restoration of a "free," that is, a profit economy, namely, that freedom can be secured only by the full restoration of private ownership of the means of production, will not be convincing during the first chaotic period of starvation and need. After this war neither the United States nor England will be able to return to classical capitalism. Their own reconstruction needs will force them to adopt measures more closely akin to a system of planning than to the economy of the nineteenth and the early twentieth centuries, and there are enough responsible groups now studying the blueprints of schemes to avoid five, ten or fifteen million unemployed. There is no way back to economic liberalism as a guarantee of freedom. After this war, liberty will require other foundations than the old-fashioned profit economy. Only those who have a plan as to how to give people work and how to start production will really serve the lasting peace.

At the same time, the freedom movement will have to defend a liberal political program, guaranteeing political and personal liberty in a planned system, against any neo-totalitarian party or group. The tragedy of this war has clearly demonstrated that without a minimum of freedom, social progress and security become impossible. The German war party, operating through Hitler's reactionary bands, could not have set the world on fire without first abolishing all liberties in Germany. Therefore, those forces which undermine freedom must be destroyed at the roots. But why should it be impossible to guarantee freedom in a socialized system? It is only in a socialized system that freedom can be permanently guaranteed in our time. The basis of freedom heretofore has resided in the civil liberties that were won in the fight for democratic emancipation and also in the relative abundance and the wealth of the democracies. Democratic rights guaranteeing the dignity and the freedom of the individual are in no way irreconcilable with a planned economic society, particularly if only such a society can promise to save people from starvation. Quite the contrary, only in such an economy can they be guaranteed. Governmental regulation alone can liberate the people from social fear in periods of depression and crisis, and so guarantee the full development of their moral and spiritual strength. In the Western democratic societies the existence of traditional civil liberties serve to lessen social fears but they alone cannot overcome them and these liberties are particularly apt to be threatened during an economic depression. It is not only fear of violence or terrorism that inhibits social progress, it may be fear of losing jobs, and the insecurity that grows out of the knowledge of cyclical depressions. Chronic fear of permanent unemployment has produced the aggressive movements that have fostered fascism in the most unstable societies of our era. There was this kernel of truth in Hitler's have-not-nation propaganda. But in the more stable societies of the Anglo-Saxon world, the chronic fear of millions of working people of losing their jobs is one of the reasons for their apathy in submitting to the rule of monopolists who are always anti-liberal and frequently favor policies contrary to the best interests of their own nation, as was again demonstrated by the maneuvers of monopolists to sabotage the war. On the other hand, a great part of the strength and the achievements of the Soviet Union, in spite of the lack of civil liberties of the Western type, can be properly understood only by realizing that its system of national planning has eliminated fear of economic insecurity. This even partly balanced the fear of state terrorism, of the purgings and treason trials. And it is this which has made the Soviet armies such an irresistible force, as has been the case with revolutionary armies at all times. Even National Socialism's war economy has demonstrated how planning and state control can overcome a depression and expand productive forces. In both systems of planning, to be sure, the constructive effects have been partly undone by the lack of freedom. The Nazi war economy lost its prestige fully when it became obvious to the German masses that the purpose of abolishing their liberties was not to eliminate unemployment, but to prepare another military assault against the world.

In Germany, some of those who look to the West for guidance will fear a planned system, while some of those who look to the Soviet Union will glorify the ideal of the Russian type of a planned economy. It will be the task of the freedom movement *equally to defend both planning and liberty;* they are not mutually exclusive. To guarantee the maintenance of liberty in post-war Germany there will have to be production of the most intensive kind geared to a system of planning. Planned economy in Germany can be a free economy, because it can be brought about by genuinely democratic and popular decision. In a defeated and pauperized Germany, coercion will not be necessary in order to explain to the majority of the people that planned reconstruction is the only way out for them. Once the old class privileges have been abolished by a free decision of the people, there will be no conflicting interests of any importance. The vast majority of the German population are productive people, two thirds are workers of all kinds. No compulsion will be needed to help a German labor government into office, by whatever political faction it is led, and there will be no insurmountable difficulties in initiating a liberal reconstruction plan under the administration of such a regime.

What people in America should never forget is that in Germany it is the workers who are the representatives of the democratic tradition. In contrast with the Western countries where the middle classes led the successful battle for civil liberties, in Germany it was the workers who fought, not only for better working standards, but also for elementary civil rights. For a hundred years, more emphasis in the political program of German labor has been given to demands for freedom of thought, freedom of speech, freedom of the press and organization than to socialism. The fact that in Russia a socialist economy has not yet been able to secure civil liberties has little bearing on the nature of the future planned economy in the West. But, even in Russia, the socialist system has brought more freedom for the productive classes than they had before the revolution. No Czarist Russia could have beaten a fascist Germany. In Germany, the traditions of state bureaucracy which found their most exaggerated expression in National Socialism are the traditions of the old ruling caste and not of the democratic movements. German socialism, like Bolshevism, by abolishing the fear of economic insecurity, will be able to free gigantic productive and moral forces. But, at the same time, it will be able to free the new society from the fear of bureaucratic terror. The lethargy and the passivity of the German people will not be overcome by restricting their liberties but by expanding them, not merely the traditional civil liberties but also freedom of organization and the freedom to join parties. Rarely can the individual defend his freedom in modern society by himself; the democratic way to defend individual rights in the highly complicated state organisms of the twentieth century is through organized groups of individuals united by mutual interests. The freedom of the individual has been and will remain the essence of democratic civilization as against autocratic barbarism of any kind. But its defense requires collective means, varying with different times and different civilizations. It is the relatively backward system of planning which is apt to be tied up with a one-party system. In Russia, limitation to one party is obviously still a heritage of the pre-revolutionary autocracy, not an inherent characteristic of socialist planning. The Russians have not yet been able to overcome their heritage. But the Russian one-party system is certainly not the only possible form of socialism, and probably not the future form in the U.S.S.R.

In fact, it is simply a unique form of transition from a backward society—a society which at the time of the revolution of 1917 was much less advanced economically and socially than Germany—to a modern socialist state. It is a mistake of the Communists to regard militant Russian socialism as the model for all socialism and to defend it as such. Just as it will be necessary to keep the defenders of the old privileges from seeming to be the standard-bearers in the fight for freedom, so also it will be necessary to take away the standard in the fight for socialism from any group trying to play the role of the vanguard of socialism by presenting an outmoded type of one-party autocracy. Only a consistent revolutionary freedom party, recognizing the rights of other parties, will be able to defend freedom and socialism alike.

A compromise of interests among the productive groups that survive the collapse will be achieved in a fair competition between various parties and organizations. This competition is natural and unavoidable. A labor party will have the greatest influence if it is fully aware of its responsibilities. It will have to defend freedom and liberty against German backwardness as well as against restrictions imposed by the occupation and against obsolete conceptions of freedom. *The legal right to organize such a party is one which is of the utmost importance to German democrats.* The most recent historical period has proved that it is just as important to the individual that the rights of political parties be guaranteed as the traditional code of civil liberties. A new bill of rights, a new charter of freedom, so urgently needed east of the Rhine, will include right of organization.

Within the political party it will be a task of the forces of freedom to defend the democratic rights of the members and to defend freedom of discussion, complete freedom of criticism, and the democratic election of leaders. In a planned economy, social discipline is needed in making and carrying out decisions, but these decisions do not need to be bureaucratic. In the work of a government-regulated economy, higher standards can be maintained than would be possible in a competitive society of the nineteenth century type if freedom of scientific thought is observed. There is no better way of meeting the real needs of the people than by putting plans before the public forum for discussion and action. It can be assumed that a system of democratic planning will emerge in spite of the fact that the international government will modify it in the apparent interests of the safety of the Allies through reparations and other adjustments growing out of international considerations. They will have a restraining effect on the system of planning, but they will not prevent it entirely.

De-Prussianization and Re-Education

It will be extremely difficult for the Germans to attain complete independence in education and in civil administration, although it is just in these concerns that self-government is most necessary.

Every discussion of "what should happen to Germany after the war" includes proposals for foreign intervention in both of these spheres. In England and America particularly, a theory has developed that the German evil can be removed only by a process of "de-Prussianization" in civil administration and by employing an expeditionary corps of foreign teachers to re-educate the youth.

The first question is one of administrative reform, specifically of limiting Prussia's influence in internal government. There is some factual basis for the theory that Prussia has had more control of domestic affairs than her size and population would warrant, but it has been grossly exaggerated because of emotional attitudes. Prussia has become a spiritual rather than a geographic reality. Actually the Weimar Republic did take some modest steps in the direction of a more proportionate regional division of administration. It did not succeed in this, however, not because the "Prussians" of 1918 were so reactionary, but because of the reactionary influence exerted by the "particularism" surviving in all of the historical German "states." This particularism was evident least of all in Prussia, which remained the bulwark of German democracy during the fourteen years of the Republic. Prussia in fact was the one state that had a relatively stable and progressive government after 1919. Its record is certainly incomparably better than that of the Bavarian government under the Republic, or, in fact, of the Reich government itself. The trouble is that from time to time quite different complexes are taken out of the box of history to illustrate "Prussianism."

Discussions in America on the future Germany, for example, seem to be dominated by conceptions that were taken directly from the archives of the particularist movements in Germany in the last century. Americans will best understand what kind of forces these were, when they remember some of the reactionary, narrow-minded anti-federalist groups and state's rights exponents in American history. Proposals are actually made for solution of the German problem by restoring archaic little states and petty monarchies which are at home today only on the musical comedy stage. The manifest purpose seems to be to eliminate the evils of Prussianism. This is one of the classic historical misconceptions of the era. After the last war all the democratic reforms originated in Prussia. It is true that Prussian militarist power had temporarily ruled in Germany, and that the old Prussian militarist tradition has to be wiped out. But after 1918 the militarists, for instance, had less influence in the Prussian government than in the Bavarian or the government of the Reich. On the contrary, it was Social Democratic Prussia that tried to resist the reactionary influences to the last minute; it was post-war Prussia that fought most consistently against rearmament. It is true that there must be reforms that will reinforce self-government and strengthen the autonomy of the regional districts. The municipalities must be given more power as must regional cooperatives. But, the way to achieve these ends is not simply to restrict the size of Prussia or to take away its powers. This is a much more complicated and subtle task which only a new German democracy can accomplish.

The real problems that will be involved in such reforms cannot be discussed until it is known how much of the old Germany will be left, in what condition it will be taken over by the post-Hitler society, and what liberties will be granted it by the occupation rulers. For the record, it should be made clear that proposals, such as those for a federalization of Germany with the recreation of conditions that existed prior to Bismarck, belong to the era of the stagecoach. Realization of such ideas would mean driving Germany back a century, politically. Such ideas are in direct conflict with hopes of "democratizing" or "Europeanizing" Germany. A program of dividing Germany up into the states of the first half of the nineteenth century would be an excellent way to create a nationalistic, revisionist and reactionary movement, a kind of ultra-Hitlerism, even if the state of Prussia were cut into several pieces. A Frenchman, General de Gaulle, recently expressed exactly the same idea in describing the nonsense of trying to "federalize" Germany by robbing it of its national unity.

The question of education cannot be considered intelligently apart from the broader question of the rebuilding of German democracy. There is only one force which will be able to re-educate the youth and to reorientate certain adult groups which were temporarily under Nazi influence. That force again is the maturing of the people themselves, resulting from a deep-rooted change in social behavior, and a democratic revolution carried to completion. That is immediately clear when we look honestly at the specific educational problems involved. As modern psychology teaches, the decisive period in building character is during the formative years of earliest childhood. Even under the Nazis, the children grow up in the family during this period. The social traditions, the teaching customs and the behavior of the heads of the family have the strongest influence on the character of the children in their first years, and consequently, throughout their lives. Even after the last war, far-reaching school reforms were carried out in Germany (they also originated mostly in Prussia) and temporarily, at least, they went a long way toward removing the influence of the traditions of the period of the Kaiser's Reich. But the revolution of 1918 left almost untouched the surviving remnants of traditional German autocracy in the family life of the middle and upper classes. And it was in those groups, where the "patterns" of the old society had been least affected, that the later reactionary and fascist infection set in. The working classes were relatively free of these influences because they had not participated equally in the "culture" of the old society. In their own organizations, their political parties, their youth movements, and their schools, they consciously began to create a democratic culture. It has been objected that the bulk of the storm troopers were drawn from the underprivileged classes. But it was primarily the uprooted, declassed paupers, not the politically organized workers, who fell for the radical movements on the right. Hitler gained many recruits from the unemployed but relatively few were men and women who had jobs in industry, or held membership in unions or workers' cultural or cooperative organizations. The majority of the impoverished men and boys recruited by the Storm Troopers had never had regular jobs, young men who never had a chance, or demobilized soldiers.

Really to eradicate the autocratic ideologies that persist in Germany will require the completion of the democratic revolution. It is from the underprivileged laboring classes that those least infected by the old society will come. No expeditionary corps of foreign teachers and no international school supervisors can have the effect that the process of democratic revolution itself will achieve.

No doubt there will be a problem also of re-education of the older classes of the youth who survive the war. But after the defeat a much greater problem will be that of combatting the waywardness and hopelessness of hundreds of thousands of young people whose youthful enthusiasm for Nazism was punctured by the collapse of the glory of the party. It should also not be forgotten that the male ranks of the youth will have been decimated on the battlefields. Their younger brothers and sisters at home, after living through air raids, evacuation and, not to be overlooked, the stultifying experience of bureaucratic Nazi child guidance, military drill and the corruption of their youth leaders, will already have been largely cured of National Socialism. Even now they do not think of the Nazi state as their state as did the Hitler Youth of 1932, but as the state of their older brothers and of their fathers. Quite in the nature of things, a conflict between generations had developed which will find its solution with the collapse of the old authority. Some pedagogues outside of Germany worry unnecessarily. A large part of the youth of Germany will be eager and useful promoters of the new society. Their grandfathers were the representatives of

Kaiser Germany; but their fathers returned from the defeat of the last war, not as supporters of the Kaiser and the old society, but as socialists and democrats. When the Republic disappointed that generation, the most active part of the younger people split off into either the communist or the Nazi opposition. It is very probable that, in reaction against the latest totalitarian authority, a new youth will come back after this war and seek new paths. Youth will not raise the fallen flag of the Nazis, youth least of all.

The teachers of Germany, having passed through and adapted themselves to several ideological periods, have lost both inner security and authority, and they will offer little assistance in the task of re-education. A new democratic youth movement will have to take a large share in responsibility for re-education itself. Recent news from Germany of growing opposition among university students, all the more significant as higher education in Germany is open only to carefully selected budding Nazis, shows that Germany has now begun to follow the path Italy took before. In Italy it has been the young people who have supported democratic and anti-fascist ideas and, as Mussolini was in power twenty years, they were children born under fascism who never had an opportunity to attend anything but fascist schools or to participate in any but fascist organizations.

As an indication of a trend away from the earlier crusading zeal manifested in American discussion about the re-education of Germany's youth after Hitler, two authorities representing two different schools of thought might be quoted from recent writings. The first is a prominent Catholic journalist and historian, the second an outstanding liberal educator. Mr. Francis Stuart Campbell in an article on "Re-Educating the Axis Youth,"* says: "The demand itself is based upon a fundamental misunderstanding of juvenile psychology in Continental Europe . . . the youth of English-speaking countries differs in certain respects radically from that of the European mainland. . . . The spirit of opposition, for instance, not undeveloped among American adolescents, is infinitely stronger in the corresponding European age-group. The teacher or professor is rarely the friend and respected adviser of the young people in his care; not only is family life in Europe more intensive, a fact which renders the educator 'suspect' as an outsider, but the secondary schools, due to their intensive program and their enervating training are hated by the adolescents with an intensity which would shock Americans. The school years for the European with his subtly anarchic sentiments is the darkest time of his life. . . . In order to transform Continentals into efficient, smoothly functioning, cooperating and 'streamlined' nations the coercive means of concentration camps, Gestapo, OGPU, firing squad, whippingpost and jail are necessary."

* *The Catholic World*, July, 1943, pages 272-273.

Re-education plans current in Allied countries are based, Mr. Campbell believes, on the assumption of a state of mind of Axis youth which has passed: "As a matter of fact Nazism as a living force among young men was at its height in Germany before Hitler came to power. . . . No self-respecting youngster [now] wants to be caught in the position of supporting the powers that-be. . . . We would be willing to go on record with the statement that not more than ten per cent of the German Youth with a secondary education are Nazis. The educational system of the Nazis is virtually a total failure. Our convictions are strengthened by news from Central Europe, and confirmed by impartial observers and students. . . . the psychological abyss between the New and the Old World, the unsurmountable philological and the linguistic differences, the personal pride of the former 'illegal resisters' who opposed Nazism courageously, all these obstacles would tend to paralyze the most sincere efforts to 'democratize' the coming European generation."

Interestingly enough in commenting on the failure of Nazi education, Mr. Campbell adds a footnote stating that the failure of systematic indoctrination "is, unfortunately, also largely true of Catholic schools in the same area; they have produced some of the worst atheists."

Mr. James Marshall, member of the New York Board of Education and formerly its Chairman, believes that the solution does not lie in Allied re-education of Nazi youth, but above all in the effort of a popular uprising in Germany. In an article in the *Saturday Review of Literature*,* he writes: "Of all the great powers, these three nations [Germany, Italy, Japan] failed to have a popular revolution.

"The reason why a popular revolution is necessary to free a people of domination is that it is the only means of freeing themselves from that form of paternalism under which they live. It is through such an upheaval that they learn the meaning of equality. This has its parallel in individual life in the period of adolescence, those years of revolt against family paternalism, those years in which normal young people acquire the courage and capacity to find satisfaction in equality and in interdependence rather than in dependence.

"When people fail to achieve this maturity they tend to remain dependent on some father-figure, some authority, and in turn to seek to dominate some one weaker, some one through whose subservience they can relieve their own subservient anxieties.

"The German father has dominated the family in the tradition of the Roman *pater familias,* in a manner and to a degree rare to the English-speaking world and to the French or Russian family.

* "What Germany Needs, A Popular Revolution Against Paternalism," *Saturday Review of Literature,* August 14, 1943, pages 8-9.

The attitude to the father is carried over to teacher, to officialdom, to the state—and now to that supreme father-figure the Fuehrer. . . .

"The most vital step, then, in bringing the German people to political and social maturity is a popular revolution which will break the tradition of the past. . . .

"The next most important step is a revision of the German educational system which, even before the Nazis, trained people for subservience to a paternalistic state—a state to be served not to serve. . . .

"A change in the emphasis of German education will undoubtedly come about if there is a revolution. It is essential even if there be no revolution. This reemphasis must be stimulated by the occupation forces of the United Nations, stimulated but not forced upon resisting victims by an army of carpet-baggers. There are many older teachers who never espoused Nazism. The young men and women who supported the recent proclamation of the students of Munich are anti-Nazi. They are to be trusted."

The re-education of adults too can be adequately handled only if there is an independent democratic movement, with its institutions in the tradition of the Folk High Schools, and with evening schools and other adult education institutions for workers.

Lastly, it should be noted that throughout recorded history educational dictatorships under foreign rulers have almost always achieved just the opposite of what they wanted to achieve.

These brief comments have only skimmed the surface of two of the most vital problems involved in self-government—civic administration and education. But they may have provided some clues for solving these problems in a democratic way and that, after all, is the way those preparing the occupation want them to be solved· The method that will succeed is to grant the *greatest possible degree of freedom and self-government.*

Special problems of international security and the problems of building parties will be treated later. The aims of the post-Hitler freedom movement may be summed up by stating that from the very start the movement will concentrate on gaining more and more responsibility and self-determination so that a modern planned economy with full civil liberties may be set up and complete national independence, limited only by the interdependence of all free nations, will finally be realized.

This struggle of German democrats for complete independence, will not arise out of nationalist feelings. It will rather be motivated by a desire for a social and democratic Germany in a European and a world system. The completion of the democratic revolution in Germany is only possible on an all-European basis. The German freedom movement will have to work in the international sphere to overcome the heritage of hatred and distrust, and help repair the devastation.

VI. The International Problems of Germany After Hitler

TO BE PEACEFUL OR TO PERISH

WHAT will be the international policy of Germany after the anti-Nazi revolution?

It may not be possible to tell what will be done with Germany at the end of the war, whether there will be a long period of probation, whether the country will be dismembered or whether there will be some milder form of temporary dependence and foreign control. But this much is certain: Germany will not within calculable time attempt to launch a war to gain revision of the defeat suffered now. It is not only that any such step must be rejected on moral and political grounds, but it would simply be impossible even under the most unfavorable peace terms. The trouble with some of the current security solutions is that they do not take sufficiently into account that the immediate problem will be more how to keep Germany going after the defeat, than how to keep her down. Immediately, certainly, there will be no need for strict controls, unless for the emotional satisfaction of people, who have suffered from Hitler Germany's aggression.

The heritage of Germany's two lost world wars cannot be forgotten even by the stupidest of all Germans. The losses of World War I had not been made up when this war began. National Socialism, itself a mass sickness and consequence of German backwardness and of 1918, has driven Germany to a second defeat which will have much more profound repercussions. At the end of this war Germany will have from ten to twenty million dead and crippled. Many German cities will be destroyed. Those industrial plants that have not been destroyed by bombings, or had their machinery carried off to the liberated countries, will need repair. Long before there had been any serious damage from Allied bombing, the Nazis estimated that, because of obsolescence and excessive wear and tear, Germany's industrial machines would require several billion marks for reconstruction and repair. Hundreds of billions of marks for war expenditures were temporarily covered by credits on future production. The new debts have gone far beyond the two hundred billion mark (220 billions marks in October 1943, not counting the billions of secret debts!) Moreover, there will be new restrictions on Germany's economic activities abroad, on her trade on the high seas, and on her acquisition of raw materials. There will also be reparations. In the most favorable eventuality, the territory of Germany will be limited to an area smaller than the Weimar Republic. Germany will have lost industries of great value and important populated areas even without dismemberment of the country. On the debit side should also be added moral loss in terms of good-will, friendship and intellectual influence. To say that Germany will be set back a half a century is to give a moderate estimate of the country's losses. Since the victorious nations, in spite of war losses, have made progress in the same period, the relative setback will be even greater. *Germany, therefore, has definitely lost out in the imperialist rivalries of the world.* That is the one immediate and positive result of the war for Germany. Germany at the same time will have ceased to be a first-class power. A realistic policy for Germany's democratic movements must, therefore, start from the assumption that for a long time Germany after Hitler will be functioning as a second or third-ranking power. This is not a position in which any group or party in Germany could plot revisionist wars, even "revolutionary" wars.

Since the defeat will be hard and the conditions severe, some Germans may have the idea that by making Germany a vassal to one of the victorious powers, or to a group of them for a period, they may eventually regain their lost prestige. The freedom movement will have to be prepared to reject deceptive opportunities along these lines that will appear most seductive but that must be avoided at all costs. Two concrete situations which might conceivably develop and tempt Germans with revisionist dreams can be envisaged. One such situation could develop if the increased power of reactionaries led to new alliances against the Soviet Union. In that case, Germany might be invited to join an anti-Soviet bloc, with promises of revision held out as inducement. It should be said at once that such a development is not probable, but it is not impossible. It will definitely not be in the interests of German progressives to act as a puppet for a reactionary international group and in so doing strengthen the genuine reactionaries within Germany itself.

The other possible situation in which Germany might turn to another power is just the reverse. Theoretically, it is not impossible that, at a given time, in the event of a conflict with the Western Powers, the Soviet Union might act to make peace conditions more agreeable for the Germans. In view of the struggle for position between the U.S.S.R. and the West, such an eventuality appears rather probable. But, in fact, it is not; it is much more likely that the Soviet Union, after the experience of this war, will try to reinforce a "security system" *against* Germany and not one that would include Germany as a part of the safeguard against Russia's present allies. At the beginning of the war there were European radicals who believed that a change in fronts, during its course, would transform the war into a revolutionary war of East versus West, following Hitler's overthrow.

As the war proceeded such ideas became patently fantastic. Recently, following the Free Germany policy in Moscow, some people who completely misunderstood the meaning of the Russian move again anticipated a change. But, even if the most improbable occurred and there was a new change of alliances, the freedom movement in Germany in its best interests would have to refuse to be included in the new conflict.

Assuming that Europe after the war should go socialist, even *in the peaceful socialist* competition Germany will find herself far down on the ladder. Her only chance to rise again in international affairs will be in the practise of a *constructive and consistent peace policy*. The only means Germany will have of combatting international influences that are not in the democratic interests of Germany and of other nations, will be the patient presentation of its case before the only existing democratic forum, the conscience of the advanced people in the world. That will be the case even after the restoration of its sovereignty.

Germany will, of course, ask for sovereignty on a basis of equality with other nations. It is understood that the national sovereignty of all nations will be limited in the future to accord with a collective security of all of them, large and small. Whenever reference is made in this book to sovereignty in the post-war situation, limited sovereignty in a system of interdependence is meant. The most perfect solution would be a federation, a united states of Europe, in a world league of all the nations of the world. This is the solution that would permit most fully the completion of the democratic revolution in Germany, and it is also the solution that would bring maximum security against some camouflaged imperialist reorganization on the pattern of the Hitler *insurrection*. A European federation and world league would make the quarantine solutions toward which most post-war planning today tends, superfluous: Quarantine solutions that envisage permanent unilateral disarmament of the vanquished Axis countries, are based on the same fundamental fallacy that has been inherent in all the solutions of power policy of all time, including the peace of 1918. When privileged and underprivileged nations are created, the poison of revisionism spreads in the latter and the poison of foreign policing in the former. Throughout the centuries of human history, time after time, the lack of stability of the power coalition has been demonstrated. There is no reason to hope for better results this time. Historically, solutions based on power coalitions have always been invitations to revisionist schemes. Power tends to corrupt, and the reactionary energies behind power coalitions are able to destroy the progressive forces in victorious and vanquished countries alike. An aggressive imperialist reorganization of Germany could be prevented most successfully by international democratic forces. The essential is to help peaceful and democratic forces within Germany herself to attain a position of influence in the reconstruction, and to prevent the emergence of German Badoglios, whether they are people like Goering or like the military crowd presented in the company of Bismarck's grandson in Moscow. The international controls which Europe, understandably, will want to impose on Germany after the experience of the last two wars, must be democratic controls if they are to be successful. They will be democratic only if Germany is incorporated in a federation, either a European or a world federation, as an equal among equals, under the supervision of the majority of the other member states. Incorporation in a larger unit, and not dismemberment in smaller pieces, is the only democratic solution.*

But it would be illusory to expect the immediate creation of such a federation, although it would be the most reasonable and the most logical solution and liberals must work towards it. There are strong forces working against a European federation and a world federation. A major difficulty is encountered in the unequal levels of political and economic development in the various European nations. The united states of Europe would not necessarily have to be united socialist states,

---

* Any German now pleading for a European federation is apt to be suspected of hidden Pan-Germanism. The author has had some bad experiences himself. Lord Vansittart, as I have already mentioned, has attacked my "temerity," but he also has questioned my motives. That is why I have included my answer to this attack in the Appendix.

but only if there are strong socialist influences in all states is a united Europe probable. The war has increased some of the objective chances for socialism on the European continent and in England, but it has also brought a setback to the champion of any socialist development, namely, the European labor movement. This setback seems temporarily so severe that even the social changes previously mentioned will not be sufficient necessarily to produce a socialist system in Europe soon after the war. Obviously the classical "socialist" parties in Europe, though they were the large and representative labor parties in their countries and not unimportant groups as in the United States, were not able to compete for national leadership in the crisis which led to the establishment of fascism in large parts of Europe—they would need deep-rooted reforms to renew themselves in order to challenge their contemporary rivals anew.

There is another difficulty in the way of the interests of the coming victors. Both the Soviet Union and England have centrifugal tendencies. Neither the British Empire nor the Soviet Union are exclusively or even primarily European powers and they are only indirectly interested in a European federation. (Recent statements in Moscow have rejected all proposals for regional European federations, and also the concept of a "United States of Europe.") Indeed there have been tentative plans for a continental federation which would exclude the two countries chiefly instrumental in bringing about the victory against Hitler—Great Britain and the U.S.S.R.! In speaking of a European federation or a united states of Europe, we mean, of course, a federation, which could not start, or develop, or exist, without British and Russian and American sponsorship. Such an agreement will not be forthcoming after the war; it is Utopian to expect it now. *It is not Utopian to expect it as the result of a development of one or two generations of peaceful resettlement in Europe, and maybe even earlier.* The United States, in spite of being sympathetic to a continental federation of states because of its own history, may be afraid that in sponsoring this federation now it will be helping to create a competitor who may possibly be stronger and more dangerous, even as a disturber of the peace, than was Hitler Germany. And finally, the smaller victims of Hitler's aggression in Europe are decidedly against a federation with Germany now, fearing that even a defeated Germany, still mighty because of her size and productive power, would through peaceful means try to get a position of hegemony in a federation of Europe. They fear that Germany would simply renew her old imperialist policy under the cover of a federation.

On the other hand, in large and small countries alike, there are trends among the advanced movements that favor a European federation. As the war is brought to an end more forces favoring federation will appear. As we have already explained,

when Hitler's economic machinery has collapsed
there will be a cry for organization on an all-
European basis. Transportation, the supplying of
food to the starving areas, the clothing of millions,
the most elementary cleaning up of the debris and
the reorganization of industries in devastated areas
—all are hardly thinkable without a European-
wide organization of the Allies. The chaos of property relations, one of the heritages of Hitler's
robberies, will drive in the same direction. Even
apologists for a complete economic restoration of
the status quo ante are skeptical of the possibility
of any legal unscrambling of the chaos. It will be
impossible to restore some of the stolen industries,
semi-legal investments of the Third Reich, to the
old private owners. Some of these owners have
been killed, others have become Nazi or Quisling
agents and will hardly survive the national liberation of their respective countries. For instance,
French industries, which were bought by the Germans with French tribute money, could scarcely
be restored to their former proprietors by the new
France. Their owners were, for the most part,
collaborationist servants of Hitler in the Ger-
manization of defeated France.

It is for such reasons that in the United States,
Fortune magazine for instance, in the spring of
1943, published plans advocating a federal European solution now. *Fortune* advocated a kind of
European protectorate of victorious European
powers, a joint occupation, the institution of a

permanent European council, a European economic authority, and various centralized agencies, such as a continental transportation office, a European air office, etc. This plan however has little chance of gaining Russian approval. It was probably inspired by the desire of certain groups in the United States to present a counter-proposal to the concepts of Anglo-Russian condominium in Europe, defended in several articles in the *London Times*, which would allow American participation with a minimum of friction. But these and similar plans for European solutions remain Utopian unless they become the common aim of the big three and such concerted agreement is unlikely for the reasons already given. All of these plans, furthermore, envisage submitting Germany to international control for a long time, based upon the belief that only after a rather lengthy period of probation, can Germany be included in a European federation or in a world league. They overlook the fundamental truth, that without equal share and responsibility, no nation will ever be won voluntarily for a project involving so gigantic a reform of the old map of the world.

The first decisive questions of national self-determination, the problems of national borders and of reparations will, therefore, have to be solved under the conditions of unilateral dependence which have been described in earlier pages.

National Boundaries

Under these conditions what attitude will the democratic movement in Germany take on the question of national borders?

First of all, it will stand for the unequivocal return of all of Hitler's annexations. The fundamental principle of national self-determination as it was developed in the period of the nation state of the nineteenth and the early twentieth centuries has been the creation of states on the basis of a national language. This principle, however, could not be applied strictly anywhere in Europe even in the former period. It was modified by historical circumstances and by the creation of stable states in which several languages were commonly spoken. Mixed language settlements have made the formation of closed national states literally impossible in many sections, particularly in eastern Europe. Furthermore, opposing interests and other powerful political factors have prevented national self-determination in the sense of the creation of clearly national states; in this way "historic" unities have developed which have not always been identical with nation states.

However, national self-determination is accepted as a democratic principle and progressive movements work towards the realization of the nation state wherever possible. Until the nation state is superseded by the federal, supranational organization, national self-determination remains an important principle. The principle of self-determination, however, implies the application of peaceful means only. Since all of Germany's expansion under Hitler came through violence, only the territory included in the Weimar Republic, the status quo ante, can be considered as the legal territory of Germany to be defended by democratic and peaceful means.

Even the first, apparently "peaceful" expansions of the Hitler Reich in German language territories were, in fact, mere conquests, achieved through political blackmail and threat of war. That was true even of the Saar Plebiscite, although it was carried on under international control which was formally not contestable. It so happened that those responsible for the international supervision were influenced by the same forces that later triumphed at Munich in the policy of appeasing Hitler's Reich. Pressure emanating from Nazi Germany influenced both the international controllers and the voters. It is immaterial that under different circumstances, for instance, if the plebiscite had been held before Hitler's victory in Germany, the Saar would more probably also have voted to return to Germany. No international decision that was taken under Hitler's pressure can be recognized by a post-war democratic Germany. The same is true, of course, of the blackmailing annexation of Austria, of the Sudeten districts, and of all the annexations that came through the direct use of the military machinery, through brutal conquest.

After Hitler, therefore, it will be the right of all the German and non-German nationalities, and the German national minorities which were incorporated by Hitler's conquest, to separate from the Reich. The new German democracy will recognize this right without reservation. The restitution of the right of self-determination to all of Hitler's victims will be the first and decisive action in determining Germany's national boundaries.

The future German democratic movement, and certainly the labor movement will, however, request that the principle of the right of self-determination also be applied to Germany itself and to German minorities outside the Weimar borders. Until a European federation is set up the German labor movement will stand for the right of German communities, outside the Weimar boundaries to decide on their own future national affiliation. Probably, some time after the defeat, after a cooling-off period, and after a certain security is established, the German labor party will demand that plebiscites take place. The most important problems will be Austria, Sudeten Germany, and the question of Germany's eastern boundary. From what has been made public in the United Nations it seems that there is already a pre-eminent decision about Austria. The idea is to restore Austrian "independence" or to incorporate Austria in a Danubian Federation. It should be honestly recognized that the Austrians themselves since the dissolution of the corrupt Austro-Hungarian monarchy have never voluntarily agreed on such independence. The independence of Austria was imposed by the treaties at the end of the last war and a majority of the Austrians were opposed to it then. Austrian people did not like the Kaiser's Germany; but their majority was inspired by the revolution of 1918 and wanted to join the Weimar Republic. They were not allowed to do so. Hitler had to come, to get Austria as a present from British appeasers. Much as German democrats have protested against Hitler's later annexation, it must be made clear that a democratic solution will be guaranteed only if, after Hitler is out, Austria gets the right to decide for herself about her future. It is up to a majority of the Austrian people to decide whether they want to be united with Germany, to be independent, or to be incorporated in a regional federation.

The solution in Sudeten German districts should be carried out the same way. Probably the Sudeten Germans would elect to remain in Czechoslovakia, because of their close economic and historical ties with their Czech neighbors. But, in a truly democratic world, it is up to the Sudeten Germans to decide this for themselves. The most complicated question will be, as it has been in the past, the problem of the eastern boundaries bordering on Poland. The German labor movement wanted to solve this age-old problem by granting to the Polish nation a safe and ample outlet to the Baltic Sea. The Corridor, however, was one of the unsuccessful products of Versailles. It did not satisfy democratic Poland and it did not satisfy democratic Germany. Even more harmful to Polish-German relations was the struggle in Upper Silesia. Later the series of accidents which gave Hitler a convenient pretext for opening the war developed around this eastern border problem. In the pre-Hitler democratic period in Germany a plan was discussed for shifting and resettling populations in the East. Such a plan might be of use for a future democratic solution of the Polish-German conflicts. But such resettlements have to be based on the principle of voluntary decisions and should not be in terms of forced transfers of populations such as we have had under fascism. Hitler's transfers were just another form of annexation.

Certain proposals for solutions that have been discussed recently, such as those advocated by the Moscow Union of Polish Patriots, would really mean the replacing of one policy of annexation by another. They will not bring security and there is always inherent in them the danger that they will encourage revisionism and permanently weaken democratic international relations. Hitler's war has, it is true, moved back the accepted moral and ideological yardsticks, and it should not surprise us to find plans for annexation presented as a means of guaranteeing security. We have the Fuehrer to thank for this as for so many other regressions into barbarism. But those who are sincerely working for a democratic movement cannot agree to such proposals.

It is premature to discuss all the questions of borders now. But it should be remembered that recent developments in Europe have again shown the explosive character of nationalism. Like all blind natural powers it acts destructively if used by forces of destruction. The nineteenth century European socialists did not always recognize the dynamic force of nationalism. But, at least since the time of Lenin, the progressive labor movement has accepted the simple, common-sense evaluation that the nationalism of oppressors is generally reactionary, whereas the desire of oppressed peoples for national freedom is generally progressive.

The Allies must decide whether they want the principle of national self-determination to give additional strength and security in the coming reconstruction period, or exert a negative influence. The scepter has been passed on to them. The German labor movement can only, patiently and persistently, bring up for discussion positive proposals to correct mistakes which may be made after this war.

It is sometimes said that the principle of the nation state has become obsolete. This is not true. Certainly it will not be until a higher principle is universally applied. As long as nation states still exist, one of the most severe disadvantages for men and women of one national language territory will be to be forced to live in the language territory of another nation. Disappointment and bitterness arising out of such settlements have been one of the headwaters of the torrent that has turned the mills of chauvinistic power policy and aggressive nationalism.

Finally, it can be said that the problems of German minorities and of other minorities after this war can never be finally and satisfactorily solved without a federal basis. These problems would lose their dangerous dynamic in a federal system in Europe. Assuming existence of a European federation, there would still be the problem, for instance, of whether Austria should be an independent member state or a province of the German member state, but it would not matter so very much. Or, considering another case, should East Prussia be a province of a German democratic state or a province of a democratic Poland? This is of minor importance if both a democratic Poland and a democratic Germany are members of a European federation. If the European constitution has a progressive social content and embraces the whole continent, then the sting will be taken out of the apparently harsh decisions that have to be made.

REPARATIONS

The second important problem for the future Germany after the lost war will be the problem of reparations. The future German labor movement will recognize that democratic Germany has extraordinary responsibilities for reconstruction in Europe and in other parts of the world. The situation is different in principle from that after the last war. It was the opinion of the European labor movement and also eventually, the opinion of an important group of American liberals, that in World War I war guilt was rather equally divided among all European power groups. This was, for example, the basic principle behind the policy of "intransigent defeatism" as practised by radical groups in Germany, Russia and some other countries during the last war. In the present war the labor forces of all countries, including the German anti-National Socialists, would not have taken their place with the Allies if they had not been of the opinion that the chief guilt for the present war resided in the aggressive imperialistic powers, that is in Hitler Germany and the Axis countries, and that to defeat them was the most immediate aim in this war.

After the last war the war guilt clause of the Treaty of Versailles, assigning sole responsibility to Germany, became the legal basis for reparations. This declaration of war guilt probably

helped more in the psychological preparation for
the present war than did any other decision of the
victors of 1918. It is, therefore, of utmost importance that the result of an impartial historical investigation of the underlying causes of Hitler's victory in Germany and Mussolini's victory in Italy
be included in the final documents of peace.
Nevertheless, it can be assumed that post-Hitler
Germany will recognize its extraordinary responsibilities for reconstruction and, further, that the
democratic movement in Germany will work for
the fulfillment of its obligations. The small nations that have suffered barbaric destruction and
the large nations that have lost so many sons and
so much property in this war will rightly demand
that Germany take a proportionate responsibility
in expiating Hitler's guilt.

Reparations to the martyred Jewish people will
be a grade A priority. This cannot be carried out
in terms of personal indemnities for there can be
no indemnification for the mass murders and the
families destroyed. Many who have escaped the
hell of the Third Reich will never want to return
and to risk a new future in their former home-
land. Therefore, a special German National Fund
for Jewish Victims should be created for the benefit of the Jewish world community, for Jewish
children all over the world, for the elderly Jewish
people who have lost their homes and their properties in Germany, for the Jewish settlements that
will be founded for refugees. In no case should

Germany after Hitler profit from the robberies of the Third Reich; in the case of the property of Jews, repayment should be made in money probably to Jewish funds and organizations. She can never make restitution for the destruction of the lives and happiness of helpless and innocent people.

However, this time too, there will be a limit to the possibilities of fulfillment. In order to keep the questions of war guilt and reparations from again becoming weapons of reactionary demagoguery within Germany, reasonable limitations will have to be decided upon. Even after World War I it was recognized that German reparations could not be the only source of repayment of war debts. At the conference of the Allies in London on March 3, 1921, Lloyd George said: "We all groan under the weight of taxes to pay our war debts. *To load all of these war debts on one country would be impossible. We, therefore, do not ask for a single mark for the cost of national defense.* (My italics. P.H.) We ask only for reparations regarding the expenses for damaged property, lives and bodies of our inhabitants." A consideration of the total costs of this war shows the importance of a reasonable assessment of reparations. There are estimates that the war has already cost Europe alone nearly five hundred billion dollars, not counting destruction from the war and not counting American expenditures. Obviously, indemnities can be paid only out of national production. National income in Germany proper before the war, reached a peak of about thirty billion dollars in the most prosperous years. After the destruction which the war has brought to Germany, it will take a long time before German production again reaches its former peak. Since only a certain percentage of the total production can be devoted to international reconstruction without destroying the capacity to produce, we again find a situation in which Germany (and the other Axis countries) would have to pay reparations for a century in order to cover only a fraction of the costs of the war. It is absurd self-deception to think such a reparations system would work. If imposed nevertheless, it could only further revisionist sentiment in Germany. Or, assuming that the strength of the Allies or of one or more of the Allies were great enough to postpone a new nationalist resurrection in Germany for generations, the mere request for reparations of the kind described, would tend to create apathy and passive resistance, and reduce the productive power left to Germany. Therefore, discussions about reparations usually take only *actual war destruction into account*. German productive power cannot be increased without some faith in a new start and in a better future for the German people themselves. Reparations claims like those imposed immediately after the last war defeat their own purpose. A democratic Germany will be ready to discuss realistic demands, and accept full responsibility for meeting reasonable obligations.

It is too early to discuss the concrete form of reparations. However, in addition to supplying manufactured goods for destroyed areas and co-operating in modernizing backward agricultural regions in Europe, this time Germany might send workers to give direct service in reconstruction. In the interests of international labor standards, the German labor party hopes to be supported by international labor in insisting on the general principle of free rather than forced labor. But if there is forced labor, such as gangs of former Nazis, they must be used with the idea of taking advantage of their productivity and not simply of punishing them. This is not to protect former Nazis. This is to protect labor standards. These gangs must not be permitted to depress working conditions for free labor. Otherwise, this method of making the war criminals pay will have a de-moralizing influence like that of colonial chain gangs or the Nazis' own methods of employing conscript labor, a practice which finally backfired on them.

Before summing up there should be a final word about future German-Russian relations from the point of view of reparations. Certainly Germany after Hitler will recognize special obligations to-wards the U.S.S.R. For many reasons: for the de-struction Hitler's army has inflicted on her; for the admiration the U.S.S.R. has won again in her heroic defense; for the merit she has acquired in destroying Hitler and so helping the German people also to become free again. Very often in discussing the value of the Free Germany Committee for German democrats, its supporters agree that the Germans would be fools not to accept an offer from the U.S.S.R. for very close collaboration. Germany and Russia would be such a perfect union. They are complementary countries with complementary markets. Russia's raw materials, her food surplus, her continuing need of machinery and machine tools, make her the ideal partner of Germany. Historically, the argument runs, this partnership was proved by the period from Rapollo until Hitler's attack. To restore it would be the only real solution of the German problem after Hitler. Not only Germans, but many Americans say this. The answer is that what truth there is in the argument about the suitability of close German-Russian cooperation applies equally under conditions of a not-exclusive relationship between the two countries. That was the case during the Weimar Republic. As long as the West was closed to Germany, she had to rely on one-sided Russian friendship and cooperation. Relations with Russia did not deteriorate, they improved, when step by step, the West was reopened to Germany. That was the case in the past. Many things have changed since. It has been explained already, that the U.S.S.R. would not offer the same preferences, politically and economically, to Germany after Hitler, as Lenin's Russia offered to Germany after the Kaiser. Among other problems in the future will be reparations. The Soviet economist, Eugen Varga, has been quoted as suggesting as suitable reparations the work of ten million German workers for ten years, which would be nearly equivalent to five billion dollars a year, if you assume one worker could produce a $500 surplus a year in excess of his living costs. Or this type of reparations might be described in terms of the proportion of Germany's working population taken away from national production. In 1929, there were twenty-three million gainfully employed; Mr. Varga's plan would thus take nearly half. Of course Mr. Varga is not the Soviet government. But this, the only reparations figure mentioned in this war, was mentioned in Moscow. There can be no doubt that the final account will be strict. In such a situation, it will be a question of death and life for Germany after Hitler not to be entirely dependent on one side, on the one big "creditor" to whom she will be indebted. In the lives of nations, as well as in the lives of individuals, such a dependence means—slavery. Enslaved nations are inert, as long as their fetters cling. They become dynamite when they see the slightest chance to revolt. *Vestigia terent.*

The international policy of the German labor movement can thus be summed up as readiness for democratic cooperation, a desire for mutual understanding, the acceptance of a full share in the work of reconstruction, and firmness in defending democratic rights. It would be to no one's advantage if vassal, dependent political parties in Germany should sign submissive documents and make promises which the reactionaries have every intention of disregarding, and which the democratic people will not have the strength to carry out. The old democratic labor movement tried to meet its obligations. Had the conditions been more reasonable in 1919, the spirit of national chauvinism would have been less successful in destroying those who signed the peace treaty of 1919 and the reparations bills that followed.*

* A CANADIAN PROPOSAL

While reading the proofs of this book an important pamphlet, "The Treatment of Post-War Germany," published by Professor R. Flenley, under the auspices of the Canadian Institute of International Affairs, came to my attention. It is too late to discuss it in this book. I should like to quote as an example of a realistic and fair-minded proposal, the suggestion for "A Realistic Peace," made in one of the sections of this symposium. The author calls it "purely imaginary," but even if imaginary, it is to my knowledge the best formulation of a possible "practical compromise" that has been made in discussions on the peace in the United Nations.

It is proposed that a defeated Germany might undertake as the price of peace:

   (a) to allow the victors to define war crimes, name the penalty appropriate for each crime, and to proceed to arrest, try, and punish war criminals who had served the Axis powers;

   (b) to pay some compensation for the use made of property confiscated in occupied countries and to allow this compensation to be assessed on terms somewhat more exacting than those considered appropriate in voluntary lend-lease transactions between allies;

   (c) to pay some compensation to civilians deliberately maimed in occupied countries and some compensation to the dependents of civilians done to death, perhaps on a scale comparable with German war pensions;

(d) to acquiesce in a rough and ready plan for restoring to its former owners equipment stolen by Germany or purchased for inadequate compensation;

(e) to allow foreign labour to return home;

(f) to cooperate in measures for "dehitlerizing" German children from (say) the ages of six to sixteen;

(g) to submit to a severe limitation of armament and to surrender, without compensation, all armaments in excess of the agreed limit;

(h) to abstain from producing armaments for an agreed period, and perhaps from producing equipment capable of being adapted to military uses;

(i) to undertake not to train men, women, or children for war;

(j) to accept economic burdens at least equivalent to the armament burdens which the victors, or some of them, will have to continue to bear;

(k) generally to cooperate loyally in all measures of international planning undertaken by the victors;

(l) to respect within Germany certain prescribed individual rights of all citizens.

In return for these undertakings we might imagine the victors agreeing:

(a) to maintain peace and guarantee Germany against aggression;

(b) to leave Germany freedom in the choice of political institutions within "reasonable" limits;

(c) to respect Germany's freedom to trade throughout the world and to restore, as far as possible, Germany's trade connections;

(d) to give, lend-lease, or lend commercially to Germany the food and equipment essential for the relief of want and for economic restoration;

(e) to accord to Germany reasonable priorities in obtaining scarce commodities during the period of relief and reconstruction, subject however to the "appropriate" priorities to be given to her victims.

If the Allied nations should offer peace in similar terms and in the same spirit, it would certainly make it easier for democratic representatives of Germany to convince the German people of a possibility of their responsible cooperation with the victors.

VII. German Labor's Mission of Freedom

DEMOCRATIC revolutions have always been carried through by large movements led by democratic political parties. And this will be the case with the democratic revolution in Germany, too. As such a party neither exists nor can exist at the present time, its development will be one aspect of the revolutionary process. In addition to the difficulties resulting from the international dependence of Germany and from the interruption in the continuity of the democratic process, there will be the problem of counteracting the shock of the one-party rule.

Modern despotism has appeared as one-party dictatorship and, therefore, something like a general anti-party feeling, a modern form of "anarchism" can be expected as a widespread reaction after the defeat of this despotism. The new democratic labor party and the other new parties in Germany, will have to emerge in an atmosphere in which there is mistrust of "party bosses," a healthy resistance to any attempt of new tyrants to get power. The entire society will be broken up into countless little groups and tiny competing authorities. Democratic parties will not be able to rise like a phoenix full grown from the ashes. On the other hand, the inital distrust of every kind of new leadership will weaken eventually just because of the need for joint action. The interests of the productive classes will help them get rid of the inverted lust for power of anti-party demagogues much more quickly than they could rid themselves of the Hitler party bosses. The experiences of the last decade proved that a totalitarian party dictatorship is only one current expression of autocracy. On the other hand, the need for disciplined democratic parties will be evident in the chaos that will prevail during the transitional period.

In the competition of the parties which will emerge in Germany, the most progressive will have the greatest effect on the society in transition. It has already been explained why the labor party would have the greatest chance of assuming national leadership.

What can be done in the way of intellectual preparation for the new labor party so that it can provide democratic leadership after the war? It is not necessary to look for an intellectual reason for the formation of this party. Parties are not only the leaders of democratic revolutions but also the organs of democratic society. The labor party in modern terms, not in the narrow guild sense of the nineteenth century, will be the party based on the traditions of the old labor movement, and in the vanguard of the new liberated mass movements.

Labor's Heritage

There is much difference of opinion about how much of this party exists now underground. Some German political emigrants, who have always over-estimated the role of spontaneity, still firmly be-lieve that after the collapse the old German labor movement will spring to life practically un-changed and take over the national leadership without an effort. Those who harbor this illusion think of the old movement as still alive; they talk about their "movement" and their "party," al-though all pre-Hitler parties and movements have been crushed to atoms. One recently wrote that the "old functionaries" will stream out of factory and shop, back from exile and up from the under-ground in "incredible" numbers. There will be no difficulty, this man believed, in the way of their presenting new leadership for the nation and or-ganizing a provisional government. There are nostalgic former German trade-union leaders who believe that it will only be necessary to cut off the head of the Hitler Labor Front to find the old free trade unions there intact. Former Social Democrats, and old Communists tend to cherish the illusion that the pre-Hitler organizations have kept on though they have really died. These old-timers forget that a new generation has grown up in the last decade. They overlook completely the frightful facts of ten years of persecution. They do not recognize that the continuity of the democratic process has been completely interrupted and are too little concerned with the tasks and responsibilities which an entirely new situation will bring.

At the other extreme there are members of the former German democratic movements who believe that everything has been destroyed. They sometimes retroactively condemn everything connected with the old movements. In the underground, these were the most hopeless pessimists; some of them were even admirers of the Nazis because "they accomplished much that we were never able to do." Abroad some of them are to be found in the camp of the neo-chauvinists, working with the Vansittartites and similar groups as German "experts," helping to discredit all of the traditions of the German past.*

Both these extremes are equally far from the truth. The critical history of the old German labor movement has not yet been written. And, without a critical evaluation of the heritage of the old movement, it will be doubly difficult to build a new one. But one can try today to point to certain roots of the failure of the old movement which are to be found in German backwardness and in the general backwardness of the progressive forces of the epoch in Europe.

There is no question that the old German labor movement was backward in relation to the task

* See Appendix 2.

before it, otherwise it would not have been defeated. But the weakness of the movement and the splits within it—often cited as the only cause of its failure—did not have their roots exclusively in the subjective mistakes of the movement. Rather, these subjective mistakes were symptoms of a more deep-seated illness, *the German illness*. The weaknesses of the German labor movement were only an expression of the backwardness of the nation whose most democratic exponent it was.

This labor movement, growing up during the period of the never completed fight for democratic emancipation, inherited a sad tradition. But, in spite of all justified criticism, one should never forget how strong that German labor movement was before the rise of Hitler, how progressive it was in comparison with the other democratic movements, and how advanced it was compared with the ruling conservatives. By studying the election figures from 1871 on we can get an approximate picture of the rise of the popular democratic forces. They grew in spite of Bismarck's anti-"Socialist Law" and in spite of the much praised virtues of the Hohenzollern Empire. Whereas, in the democratic countries the ruling class has generally considered the labor movements as a part of the political life of the nation in spite of bitter conflicts, in Germany such was not the case. The semi-feudal and the militaristic ruling cliques turned savagely against every democratic force and most of all against labor. In fact, Wilhelm II labeled almost half the nation as "enemies of the Empire." (That did not, however, prevent some labor bureaucrats from being loyal "Kaiser-Socialists" up to the time the Republic was established. Later, under the Republic, this same minority among the labor leaders became the errand boys of the *Reichswehr* even to the point of voting for the pocket-battleships.)

Although German democrats were always at variance with the ruling class, nevertheless, the democratic movement and its leaders in particular naturally were influenced by the general character of German society. Like the liberalism of the classical period, German Social Democracy was stronger in words than in deeds. Not free of autocratic influences in its own organizational structure, the democratic movement in its struggle to defend and expand democracy, manifested a "parliamentary cretinism" which was indicative of the essential political impotence of its leaders. There were pseudo-scientific influences in its literature and the training of its members was doctrinaire in some respects. The Social Democratic party never entirely outgrew the backwardness of German philosophy during the period when it was founded. The followers of LaSalle contributed their predominantly autocratic organizational ideas while the petty bourgeois labor clubs were tainted by the influence of "Eisenacher." The "Marxism" of German Social Democrats, so bitterly fought by the reactionaries, was often only a vulgar Marxism, a kind of fatalistic pseudo-religion, including faith in the inevitability of a future victory to be determined purely by economic factors. Opposition groups were easily expelled from the party, beginning with the liquidation of the so-called "youth" and leading up to the hounding out of the left wing and the eventual break away of the Independent Socialists during and after the last war. The rather autocratic color of the party leadership remained even after the collapse of 1933 and its vestiges can be found in the last remnants of the party that survive today. Nevertheless, in its mass character and pretty largely in its aims and its programs this movement was democratic. Compared with the rest of the parties in Germany, with the Catholic Center party, for example, which is so often praised today, the Social Democratic party was like a one-eyed man among the totally blind.

The German Social Democratic movement might have been able to live up to its responsibilities if the split following the last war had not robbed it of so large a share of the forces needed for its regeneration. The process of decline started when the Independent Socialists split off from the parent party. When a part of the Independents joined the Communists in a competing party, the Social Democrats lost their influence for good in certain key groups of industrial workers. The new Communist party, on the other hand—the result of a subsequent split in the ranks of the Independents, due to Moscow's illusions and the help-lessness of the right-wing leaders of the Independents—contributed to the deterioration of the entire movement. Among its members were some of the keenest and best political minds among the workers of Germany. The split in the German labor movement was not primarily the handiwork of the radicalism of revolutionary Russia. It started before the Russian revolution as the separation of the Independent Socialists during the war proves. It was pacifism which started the split, not Bolshevism! But it was Russian influence that made it permanent. The Russian Communists then believed in world revolution and they were especially confident that they could bring about revolution in Germany with the help of a party of their own. But the German Communist party would never have become a mass party if the chronic economic crisis after 1918, the Treaty of Versailles, and the bureaucratic incompetence of the Social Democrats—the largest party in the Republic—had not aided the competing Communists. The Communist party, though dependent on Russia, and doctrinaire and anti-democratic in its methods, was in reality a distorted section of the democratic movement, robbing it of strength in the hope of recreating it in its own image. It started as a genuine radical anti-war party; later it got under the influence of Russian dogmatism and autocratic ideologies. The conception of "the role of the party" was autocratic and so was the effort to make this party omnipotent. The Communists suffered from the fanaticism of a sect with a compulsion to impose its ideas and its policies on the entire movement. The Communist party felt it had to dominate, but being too weak for that it reinforced its self-confidence by a chronically belligerent attitude which merely stimulated antipathy and resistance from others. The result was that the party was in a constant state of irritability and hurt feelings about actual and imagined persecutions. Thus it discredited the progressive ideas for which it had originally wanted to fight.

As early as the revolution of 1848 a similar kind of dogmatism emerged, a manifestation of the immaturity of the early democratic movement. The group around Marx, the revolutionary democrats of 1848, who were known as the Communist League, criticized the most dogmatic groups of that time, the Schaper-Willich faction, in the following words: "for you, will-power alone turns the wheels of history." The Communist League kept the doctrinaire groups from "modeling" the whole movement according to their dogmatic ideas. The revolutionary democrats of Marx's group believed "subjective idealism," as they called the leftist radicalism of this period, to be a carry-over from the autocracy of reactionary society. After the November revolution in 1918, "subjectivist" tendencies developed again in the radical movement in Germany, this time as a mass movement—the Communists. There were no highly-qualified revolutionary democrats to set them right as the leaders of Marx's "Communist League" had set the Schaper-Willich faction right seventy years before. When the depression of 1929 came, the radicalism in Germany, both indigenous and imported, lacking in independence and retarded, came to the end of its long resistance and fell victim of the National Socialist counter-revolution. The real "subjectivism" finally found its complete flowering in the fascist party rule.

There are psychologists today who want to explain the "German evil," the dominance of autocratic ideas, in psychopathological terms as "paranoia." In making such a diagnosis the psychologists overlook the fact that there is little that is specifically German in the autocratic ideologies. We find similar manifestations in all countries and at all times when class conflicts became acute. The content of the ideologies may vary, but the apparently neurotic character is always present. In our era we find that such ideologies usually develop in countries where the democratic process is backward as in Germany and Japan. Being essentially autocratic, they can never serve progressive movements. Autocratic ideologies may develop in radical movements but they distort those movements; they are always, in effect, weapons of reactionary groups. The fact that there was mass support of autocratic conceptions in both left and right-wing radical groups in Germany showed not only how far behind the democratic process was after the last war, but also how unstable the new Germany was, and how superficial was its apparent health, before its complete regression became evident with Hitler's advent to power. In analyzing the backwardness of the democratic labor movement in Germany, it also should not be overlooked that after the last war, and again in the depression at the end of the twenties, the entire structure of European democracy received a profound shock. Not only the German labor movement, but practically all the labor movements of Europe showed in these crises that they were not strong enough for the tasks that faced them. In almost all countries there was immature radicalism on the left and obsolete opportunism on the right. The Germany story in 1933 was certainly no worse than the collapse of French labor in 1939–1940. The French movement, however, revived more quickly and has become a vital sector of the national defense against the Nazi oppressor.

The collapse of the Hitler system alone will not bring Germany up to date. That is all the more true because the Hitler war has reawakened those reactionary forces in Europe which will influence the future of Germany. The coming German democratic movement will be affected by the heritage of the past. It cannot be predicted how much influence the neo-communist movement will have (in spite of the dissolution of the Comintern) and how negative and immature the new movement will be. That will depend on the international situation and especially on the role Russia will play. We must again be aware of the extraordinarily great influence the Soviet Union will exercise after this war, no matter what transformations it goes through and what the relative weight of its influence in the councils of the Allies. There is no question, certainly, that it will have particularly great influence on mass movements in Germany after the war. One of the most important tasks will be to cultivate friendly relations with the new Russia that emerges from this war, and at the same time one of the most difficult problems confronting a democratic party in Germany will be to combat the negative aspects of its influence. A "hard" peace, for whose imposition Russia was co-responsible, no matter how it hurt Germany, would weaken its influence on the democratic movement. On the other hand, if the Soviet Union turns out to be the only force to offer the German people an alternative to destruction, allegiance to the U.S.S.R. would be almost inevitable. In any case, the democratic movement must be better prepared intellectually than it was in 1918 to combat the infantile disease of neo-radicalism. Only thus can a new splintering of the movement be prevented.

The old labor movement in Germany had gone further in its thinking than Western liberalism. That does not mean that German labor people cannot even today learn from Jefferson and Lincoln and from English liberalism. It was true in the old movement, and it will be even more true in the post-Hitler movement, that the problem is to make use of the great heritage of Anglo-Saxon liberalism for the new period and for special German conditions. As far back as the end of the last century it was clear to labor that in Germany, unlike the Western countries, the middle classes could not bring liberal emancipation, that the workers had, by destiny, been assigned that task. It was also clear that this emancipation was no longer to be achieved through the development of private initiative in a "free" bourgeois economy, but only in a socialist economy. It can be expected, however, that after the war, assuming that Western armies of occupation are in the country, Western influences and ideas, partly in religious form, will also play an important part in Germany. It is of paramount importance that the new movement must never forget its own democratic mission and never forget that, in securing real freedom in Germany, final insistence on a Bill of Rights east of the Rhine is just as necessary as socialism. The democratic revolutionaries, that is, the German socialists, will, of course, interpret their "four freedoms" in accordance with their own conditions and their own needs. But in Germany these freedoms can be guaranteed only by a democratic-socialist society. State planning must be the servant and not the

master of that new society. The democratic party
or parties must be the devoted guardians of the
democratic revolution. But, on the other side,
there seems to be no basis for democracy without
this "socialism." After the overthrow of the Nazis
and the destruction of the old ruling class conditions in some respects will be more favorable for
setting up such a society than they were in 1918.

THE LABOR PARTY OF TOMORROW

The new democratic labor party of Germany
cannot simply come into being as the continuation of the old labor parties, or through the merg-
ing of their remnants. The ideas of 1848, of 1871,
of 1917 or 1932, will not be adequate for the new
problems. Nor can the old officials and the old
party members master the new responsibilities.
The officials of the Comintern must have been
aware of that fact when they decided upon dissolution, thus renouncing their claim to being the
avant garde of the movement. For twenty-five
years it had been one of the greatest obstacles in
the way of a reorganization, a new formation of
the entire movement. This decision will be a help
in preparing the new movement. It will make it
easier for many courageous communist workers in
the underground groups to break their old ties
with the totalitarian tradition. It will make it
easier for them to understand the young, non-

communist movement, even to join it. However, important as will be the part played by surviving members of the various former groups who carried on during the first period after Hitler's fall —and the old Communists cannot be discounted because many of them have shown heroic resistance to Hitler—they are not the ones who will determine the character of the new society. Only those who were able to adapt themselves and learn, and who have the strength to begin anew will be able to make a real contribution. But since the strongest force in shaping the new movement will be the experience that the people had in opposing Nazism in Germany under Hitler rule, the central place in the new movement will be occupied by the young militants of the underground. The movement's greatest lack will be in young party officials with modern ideas and, even more, of experienced modern party leaders. In building up the party, therefore, especial care must be taken in training new staffs. And the most important of all tasks in the reconstruction is that of developing a highly-qualified corps of active members. Efforts must be concentrated on aiding talented young people to come to the fore, and on recruiting potentially able people from among the numerous "partisans," the veterans, of the underground movement.

Unconditional freedom of intellectual association, freedom of discussion and criticism, is the other prerequisite for the development of an up-to-date corps of responsible people in a party, and, finally, the conscious cultivation of tolerance and comradeship as they have developed in the underground. These liberties and these free democratic ties must be scrupulously observed at the same time that the necessity for discipline in action is recognized. The party will have to demand the greatest material and moral sacrifices from its members if it hopes to create out of the depth of the collapse the strength for a new start. Hundreds of thousands, millions, of inadequately trained people will have to take responsible positions as representatives of the democratic movement, positions which were previously filled by the autocratic elite and by the Nazis. They will include positions in political and economic organizations, in the new trade unions, in the new cooperatives, in the cultural organizations and in the civil service. If labor hopes for success in democratic rivalry with the other new parties, it must concentrate on the quality of its membership. This is necessary if the party is to develop new leaders with democratic authority and to eradicate the heritage of autocratic bureaucracy.

Thus it is clear that certain widely held conceptions are false, for instance, the idea that the Labor Front could be transformed back into free trade unions simply by removing the Nazi leaders and replacing them with former trade unionists. By the same token, artificial attempts to create "Unity Party Committees" out of members of the emigration, and to name "Provisional Representatives," will not further the work of the future movement. An abundance of Free Germany Committees of exiles may be useful, in some respects, but will mean little for the comeback on the inner front. It is more constructive to train future members and helpers in critical thinking, in the use of modern scientific methods, and patiently and carefully to combat the vestiges of the old dogmatism and intolerance, than it is to manifest a great deal of activity in drawing together remnants of the past. The activization of whatever remnants of the party abroad are still vital and capable of development will come as soon as a new democratic movement has developed within Germany itself.

The emigration has useful work to do in preparation for the future, e.g. in assembling, choosing, and training the men and women in the emigration who want to put themselves at the disposal of the movement, and who can better prepare their return home in a joint, organized fashion than individually. Another important task is to continue attempts to make contact with the country, difficult as it may be, in view of the splits and the weakness of the groups abroad and the restrictions under which they must work. Though there is little chance of success, the attempt should still be made to get permission for recruiting among German war prisoners in Western countries, who, as is now known, include many ardent anti-Nazis. Such preparatory actions have more chance of success if there is unity among the emigration. But, the emigration should not be overestimated: it is only one factor in the preparation of the new democratic freedom movement—not the strongest, but the weakest.

The Allies, mostly aware only of the emigration in their midst, should also be aware that the real German partners for a coming democratic world are inside Germany. If, through the defeat of Hitler, revolutionary energies are set free, the forces which are in a position not only to begin a new life but to help build a new state with modern democratic goals will come particularly from among the younger people in the liberated movement at home.

Returning emigrants can be of some constructive help to the new movement in Germany; they will bring contacts with groups abroad, they will bring the knowledge they have gained in other countries.

It has been less than a hundred years now since the first independent beginnings of a modern labor movement in Germany. Historically, a century is a short time. In those countries in which the process of bourgeois emancipation was completed, it took much longer than a century. In Germany, the completion of this process is the mission of the labor movement. There were some workers' societies prior to 1848, but it was not until 1864 that the first larger political labor societies grew up in Germany, precursors of the later labor parties. Since then there have been about thirty years during which the growth and development of the labor movement was interrupted by violence: the period of the (anti-) "Socialist Law" under Bismarck, the period of the World War, and the Hitler regime. The modern German labor movement has had therefore about fifty years altogether in which to develop in comparative freedom. That is a very short time. There were, it is true, many German socialists who, in 1918 thought that the realization of the labor movement's aims was near. No one expected the deadly blow and setback that fell eleven years ago. No one can predict today how long it will take to realize those aims and what difficulties will first have to be overcome. But today no one can quite measure the tremendous liberating effect which the defeat of fascism will have. Though one must anticipate a hard time during the period that post-Hitler Germany is dependent on outside forces, and has to fight its way through, there is still reason to hope that the German labor movement will fulfill its mission, and that after the terrible blows of the Hitler time, when the Nazis have been overthrown, it will forge ahead.

VIII. The Glacier Recedes

WHEN this war came, the world at large was unprepared. Now with the end of the war in Europe approaching, the world at large again is unprepared. Peace and desire to keep peace had made the democratic world unfit for war. The war into which it was plunged and which has absorbed all of its energies has made it somewhat unfit for peace. The new adjustment will be difficult. Like an expanding glacier the ice masses sent out by the world centers of reactionary fascism had penetrated deeply in the regions of happier political climates. Now, as the glaciers recede, they leave behind them moraines and the cooler climate of a transitional period which will last until the ice is fully broken up in the reactionary centers from which it first expanded. There can be no doubt that the columns of pioneer armies that are following along the line of retreat of the glacier through Africa and Italy (a retreat that is faster than was expected) have not been rightly equipped politically for the sudden change. It found them unprepared. The Italian people wanted to return to the summer raiment of democracy. They were offered the old, somewhat moth-eaten furs of the

House of Savoy and Badoglio. Again another break in the ice is imminent: Central Europe is going to be cleaned up soon. And, again the right equipment is not available.

It is later than you think. Of course the complete adjustment will take a longer while and some shortcomings can be overcome in the transition period. It will be possible to correct mistakes, but only after finding out in time how great is the danger of making fundamental and irretrievable errors. The Nazi government secretly through indirect channels asked for armistice terms for the first time in September 1943. Of course it would not admit this. The U.S.S.R. is said to have demanded that the Nazis retire behind the old German borders in the East and deliver Hitler's head before any negotiations could be considered. Once more the Nazis assembled their last strength to hold out for better terms, hoping for some opening through a conflict among the Allies. Any time now the first maneuvers towards peace may start since the Nazi hopes for a separate peace were buried at Moscow.

Russia was better prepared for war when it came; she is better prepared for the decision to come now than the West. This is the simple, uncontestable truth behind all the recent controversies. The U.S.S.R. has made an offer to Central and Western Europe which is essentially more liberal than the offer of the democratic West has been. Hitler and Goebbels try to capitalize on this dissension. Time and again they have said, "We or Bolshevism." They say it again now, the last-ditch defense campaign begun under the slogan, "Our Victory or Bolshevism." This is of course only a last big lie. There is no more an alternative —Nazi victory or Bolshevism—because a Hitler victory is out of the question and Hitler knows it. Hitler rose to power under the same slogan and it was a lie then. The alternative at that time was: Hitler or German democracy. The alternative now is: a Russian political victory in Europe or a joint United Nations victory in Europe that will make a German democracy possible.

The greatest difficulty for the achievement of a joint victory at present is the political lag in the West. There is very little time left to throw out the obsolete political equipment which has piled up for several years. In this equipment one of the most outdated weapons is the idea of "legitimacy" taken from the Metternichean museum, another is the Vansittartite idea about the incapacity of the German people for democracy, their innate evil qualities as a race and a people. It is one of those infiltrations of archaic ideas which penetrated the West under the pressure of the threatening and expanding fascist glacier. Essentially it is the exact duplicate in reverse of Hitler's own tribal and racial doctrines. It was a part of his warfare to infect his enemies with his own poison. The unprecedented brutality and ruthlessness with which the German people as a whole, being Hitler's coerced soldiers, have waged the war, has made it easier for the Hitler poison to penetrate people's minds. It is difficult to get rid of the poison. But the mind of the West must get rid of it in order to make a strong and sober peace. There is only one strong peace, a democratic peace. One prerequisite is the re-establishment of common-sense judgment about what the German people are. If Hitler, and his counter-parts on the other side, contend that the German people are different from all others, it is necessary to go back to the simple truth that they are exactly like all others, not better, of course, and hardly worse. It should not be difficult for Americans to accept this notion, which is implicit in American civilization.

Germans have been a part of the American community since Colonial days. In the eighteenth and nineteenth centuries Germans came to American shores as religious emigrants, fighting for freedom of worship; some of their descendants, still known as Pennsylvania Dutch, are certainly among the most pacific elements in America. Germans came to this country again as political emigrants after the 1848 revolution had been defeated in Germany. In the American Civil War some German names were rallying cries in the crusade against slavery, Carl Schurz for example. A new wave of political emigrants opposed to Hitlerism has only recently arrived. All of these immigrants, from the Mennonite to the anti-Nazi were of the Teutonic "race," and they have contributed as much to

American life as have immigrants of other national origins.

There is enough historical understanding among the people of the melting pot to remember that Scandinavians who are so often and justly admired for their advanced state of civilization, were once more ruthless than the Huns, in the period from the days of the Vikings to the Swedish ravagers of the shores of the old continent; that the British have not always been the highly cultivated nation they are today but have practised piracy, robbery and other vices around the globe; that later, the French—less than 140 years ago, during the Napoleonic wars—invaded all of Europe. Napoleon reached even farther into Egypt and Russia than Hitler ever did; the French then, in the opinion of their contemporaries, were the hated Huns as the Germans are today. That was how the British who were threatened with invasion, as today, felt, and also the Germans whose territory Napoleon made one of his battlefields. All of them have been tamed, Scandinavians, British, French and the others. There is no reason why this should be impossible in the case of the Germans. To be sure, it has always been difficult for the sufferers and the contemporary victims of the aggressors to produce at the same time the strength for defense and the wisdom for effective treatment of the aggressor. It is more difficult than ever now. Two devastating wars in which the German leadership has committed more extensive crimes and com-

manded greater power temporarily than any conquerors in previous history have left deep wounds.
That is why the cry for security is now worldwide.
But this again offers on the other side a great
chance for a real and enduring solution. This
book has tried to sketch an outline of such a solution, as envisaged by the German victims of German aggression. If it is true that for certain
definite reasons German democratic development
has been delayed, that neither the racial character
nor long-run historical traditions hinder the final
democratization and civilization of the Germans,
then the task is to sponsor and encourage the completion of the democratic revolution in Germany.
Of course that implies a complete change in German leadership, a complete replacement of her
"elite" by new democratic leaders. But it also
needs a revision of the earlier peace plans of the
West. The Allied solution will be a good one if
it permits a deep-rooted revolution in Germany.
It will not work if it does not permit that. A vin-
dictive or solely punitive solution of the German
problem will not solve it and will not give security
to the world. Only a democratic solution of the
German problem is the proper one. If Germany
cannot be offered participation democratically in
government immediately, this participation must
be offered symbolically, with the "empty chair"
left empty, in all sincerity, to be taken by German
democratic representatives later in local, national,
European, and world government. This is the

only way to strengthen what is healthy in Germany itself, to strengthen the weaker partner; perhaps he will not really be as weak as expected.

Are the German people able to cooperate?

There can be no doubt that millions of people in Germany have considered the Nazi regime as a reign of terror; as a party, not as *the* German regime; that, like other victims of the Nazis, they have hoped and expected to be liberated. If the victims win their confidence, their cooperation, their enthusiasm, for a constructive solution, that and that only will eventually allow Germany again to take her place among the civilized nations. This will create a spirit of cooperation necessary to make amends for the past and make it possible to develop that specific genius of German organizational, technical and productive capacities, which will enable Germany tomorrow, for the first time in history, to take her useful place as an equal among equals in a free society of nations. This is the only way to stop German agression once and forever.

Appendix 1

Munich Student Manifesto

"Fellow Students!

"Our nation stands shaken at the spectacle of the destruction of our men at Stalingrad. The ingenious strategy of the World War corporal has driven 330,000 German men to a useless death. Our Fuehrer, we thank thee.

"There is a ferment among the folk of Germany. Do we want to continue to entrust the fate of our armies to a novice? Do we want to forfeit what is left of our young people to the depraved lust for power of a party clique? Never again. The day of reckoning has come, the day of reckoning of our German youth with the most despicable tyranny under which our people has ever suffered. In the name of the entire German nation, we demand that Adolf Hitler's state give back to us the most precious possession of the German people, which he stole from us—our personal liberty.

"We grew up in a state in which every free expression of opinion was ruthlessly gagged. Hitler Youth, Storm Troops, S.S. have put us into uniform and crippled our intellects during the most fruitful period of our lives. They call their contemptible methods 'training in *Weltanschauung*,' but the purpose is only to stifle any budding of independent thought or independent judgment. A more devilish or a more limited leadership than ours is inconceivable; the future party bosses are trained to be godless and unscrupulous exploiters and murderers, to be blind and stupid followers. We 'intellectual workers' are only good enough to act as policemen for the new ruling class. Fighters at the front are treated like schoolboys by student leaders and Gauleiter candidates. Lascivious Gauleiters molest the honor of women students. The men stood up for their feminine colleagues. The students at Munich University have given a worthy answer. It is the beginning of our battle for free self-determination, a beginning that is not without spiritual value. We owe a debt of gratitude to those brave students for the inspiring example they have given us.

"We have only one slogan! Fight against the Party! Get out of Party organizations, where they hope to strangle us politically. Keep away from the S.S., from the Party leaders and their satellites. Our interest is in true scholarship and in genuine freedom of spirit. No threats can frighten us, even threats of closing our universities. Everyone of us is fighting for his future, for his liberty and his honor in a state which will recognize its moral obligation.

"Honor and liberty. For ten years Hitler and

his comrades cruelly twisted, distorted and ridiculed those two fine German words, as only unscrupulous men can, who throw the highest values of a nation to the swine. What honor and liberty mean to them they have demonstrated clearly enough in the ten years in which they have destroyed all the material and spiritual freedom, and all the moral substance of the German people. The horrible blood bath in which they, in the name of the liberty and honor of the German nation, have plunged all Europe, and which they daily perpetuate, has opened the eyes of even the dumbest German. The name of Germany will be shamed forever, if German youth does not finally rise to take revenge, to destroy its tormentors and create a new Europe, a Europe of the spirit.

"Students! The German people are looking to us. They expect much of us. Just as in 1813 Napoleon's terror was broken, so in 1943 the National Socialist terror shall be broken by the strength of the spirit. Beresina and Stalingrad are aflame in the East. The Stalingrad dead implore us: Forward my people, follow the torch.

"Our people are rising against the enslavement of Europe by National Socialism, in a new breakthrough for liberty and honor."

Appendix 2

IN his recently published book, *Lessons of My Life,* the Right Honorable Lord Vansittart, P.C., G.C.B., G.C.M.G., D.Litt., LL.D., devotes a good part of a chapter to what he calls the "crypto-pan-Germanism" of the "extreme German Left." He illustrates his thesis by reference to the writings of some of these "Left Wing, pseudo-intellectuals. . . . accomplices of Tirpitz!" He writes: "I have in my possession a copy of a pamphlet published in Paris in July 1939 under the title of *Der kommende Weltkrieg*—The Coming World War. The authors belong to a group called *Neubeginnen,* to the Socialist Workers' Party of Germany and the Revolutionary Socialists of Austria. Being German, they prefer complication to simplicity. They therefore readily accept the Marxian sophistication that any war is essentially a clash between economic antagonisms. Therefore this one must be the inevitable result of 'the inner laws of development of the capitalist system itself.' It has never occurred to them that there is so simple and dreadful a thing as a national lust for power. They appear unconscious that such a lust may obtain even under a Socialist regime, and then proceed to demonstrate that in German and in Germany even this is not only possible but easy.

"They did nothing effective to stop Hitler or to start a revolution; but when once the war has broken out, they expect us to do what they did not attempt, to dethrone Hitler and to install them—in order that they may lead not only Germany but Europe, the world. The Germany which they will monopolize will take charge once more, but in revolutionary garb. 'The Socialist Revolution in Germany will be the next decisive link in the chain of World Revolution.' The new German hegemony is based on the old grounds that Germany is 'the most highly industrialized country in the Old World'; that 'the historical and cultural conditions of Germany,' and the 'general educational and cultural level' of the masses entitle them to take precedence over lesser breeds—such as the Russians. (Another echo of Marx.) They even invoke in support the German 'democratic traditions,' which have never shown any sign of life. On these hoary fictions German 'revolutionaries' never tire of reiterating German claims to dominate by sheer German virtue. Weaker countries may, if they so choose, decline to federate with Germany—but only in theory. In practice 'the people of Central and Eastern Europe live so inextricably mixed together that any attempt at drawing frontiers on these lines [of self-determination] would be attended with the greatest technical difficulties. And in addition many of them are so small that their national States would not be able to exist independently.' This is getting uncomfortably near Frederick II and 'unjustified existences.' ''*

From these quotations, one would assume the pamphlet gives an alarming picture of German megalomania and even worse, of German stupidity. Although the pamphlet is unsigned and was published as the product of discussions among individuals affiliated with certain German underground labor groups, the British Lord reveals the names of two men to whom he attributes authorship. One is Paul Sering a German refugee now in London and the other is the author of this book. I do not want to take undeserved credit. The truth is that I wrote only a very small part of this pamphlet, and can make no claim to authorship of the sections referred to. I did take part in the discussions in Paris in 1939 which led to the writing of the pamphlet. Moreover, not only was I completely in agreement with the document at that time, but today after so many years, I still find it correct in many basic ideas, which is rather amazing for a political treatise. It shows an understanding of political developments that few of its con-

* Lessons of My Life, by Lord Vansittart, pages 85-86.

temporaries possessed though, of course, in many points events have rendered it out of date.

But two quite different documents are under discussion. The one for which I am jointly responsible, "Der kommende Weltkrieg"* ("The Coming World War,") is a document expressing the desire for peace and freedom of the underground German labor movement. It has never been translated into English. The other of which Vansittart speaks is a document of "crypto-pan-Germanism." It is a collection of quotations, halves of sentences and sometimes only words, sought out in the text of the real pamphlet and fitted into a new order. It is a kind of jig-saw puzzle in reverse. Words and sentences are taken out of context and fitted in where they suit the picture that Vansittart is zealously painting of Germany in general and of the Germans, left and right. It is from this imaginary pamphlet that Vansittart quotes. To illustrate the process of transforming document No. 1 into document No. 2, here is an example. Imagine that you should hear a report about a dangerous defeatist in our midst, an American who said the following: "We must sell our newly-built merchant marine to more farseeing powers, crush utterly, by embargo and harassing legislation, our foreign trade, close our ports." Who said that? You will not believe me when I tell you that President Roosevelt made these remarks. It was in a speech delivered in 1920. But, of course, the entire sentence is not

* *Der kommende Weltkrieg*, privately published, Paris, 1939.

quoted and the context is not given. The President actually said: "We must either shut our eyes, sell our newly-built merchant marine . . . or we must open our eyes and see that modern civilization has become so complex as to make it impossible to be in this world and not of it." In the case of the President such a misrepresentation is not taken seriously. In the case of an unknown author it is quite a different matter.

I have to take the trouble to play the puzzle game backwards, and place all the little parts that Vansittart took out and put together in different meanings to make an imaginary pamphlet back in the right context in the original. This will not be easy as the pamphlet is forty-two pages of small print.

The first chapter of "The Coming World War" describes the damage which the advance of Nazism *and* the appeasement policy of the great European powers of that time did to the labor movement of Western Europe and to the underground democratic forces in Germany, in Italy and in the countries that were already oppressed by fascism as well as in the small nations that were threatened. (The pamphlet was published half a year after Munich.) This chapter points out, regretfully, how weak the progressive forces were in the anti-Hitler front that was forming then. But the authors state explicitly that they consider themselves members of that front. The pamphlet says: "That the progressive factors within the anti-

Hitler coalition are weak today, that they have shown themselves incapable, on their own and under their own leadership, of bringing an anti-Nazi front into being, that the French Popular Front has remained only an episode, are effects of fascist expansion itself. Therefore, the pre-war period is a period of the most grave international reaction for the reason that the international advance of fascism gives it its stamp."

The fact that the progressive forces were so weak then made it all the more important to the writers of this pamphlet that Hitler should be beaten. The obvious corollary was that a German revolution—remember, Europe was not yet at war —was the key to encouraging and strengthening the progressive forces of Europe. One of the characteristics of the coming world war will be "the key position of the German revolution in regard to the beginning of the coming wave of revolutions"; it will, says the pamphlet, be "the reverse of the key position of German fascism for the advance of international reaction."

This estimate of the key role of the German revolution, in a reversal of the trend from further expansion of fascism to its defeat and to the beginning of a new democratic era, is further elaborated in the second section of the first chapter entitled, "For the Defeat of Fascism." There is a detailed analysis of why the defeat of German fascism is the decisive prerequisite for further progressive development anywhere, including the countries of the anti-Hitler front of that period, England and France. At the time the pamphlet was written that was not nearly so clear as it is now, especially not in France, as we have since learned, but also not in England.

The second chapter, "The Goal of German Socialists in the Period of Revolutionary Transition," proceeds from this idea. It lists immediate aims: the destruction of the Nazi machine, the reorganization of the system of economic planning on the basis of popular needs and, thirdly, the guarantee of democratic liberties. The pamphlet continues: "As fascist Germany was the center of world reaction, so *the socialist revolution in Germany will be the next decisive link in the chain of world revolution.*" Here, at last, we have dug out the first literal quotation presented by Vansittart. But here it looks different. Here there is not the slightest similarity with the idea that Germany is the center of the world, the idea from which has sprung the German claim for world hegemony. Turn it around as you like, and you will find no pan-Germanism in it. We say that a democratic revolution in Germany will have as much strategic importance in determining the relation between progressive and reactionary forces in the world as German fascism had. Hitler was the center of world reaction, Vansittart will not deny that. Break Hitler and Germany's revolution will be the next link in the chain of developments toward a progressive era. What is wrong with that?

Where is the crypto-pan-Germanism? In order to prove that we claim hegemony again for Germany Vansittart is content to cite the second half of an original sentence without reproducing its context, without even explaining that it is only half a sentence.

He also accuses us of the commendable expectation of getting this revolution handed over to us by the Allies, after they have shed their blood to beat Hitler: "They expect us to . . . dethrone Hitler and install them—in order that they may lead not only Germany but Europe, the world." We have never thought of or said such a thing. On the contrary, those responsible for the pamphlet belong to that section of German anti-Nazis which is opposed to puppet governments, whether they are supported by rightwing or leftwing foreign governments. Also we have never succumbed to the illusion that the conservative leaders of the Western Powers would prefer a revolutionary group in the saddle in Germany. At the time the pamphlet was written their names were Chamberlain and Daladier! Both the author's present book and the earlier pamphlet are quite clear on this point. "The Coming World War," in describing the anticipated actions of the Western Powers in conjunction with German reactionaries after Hitler's defeat says: "They will try to replace Nazism by a military dictatorship based on German and foreign bayonets. In case that fails, they will at least try to salvage the special position of the military apparatus as in 1918. In the name of the *Rechtsstaat* and of law and order they will try to stabilize a new constitution, if necessary even a democratic one, before the revolutionary movement has created basically new power conditions. Every blow against the beneficiaries of the Nazi dictatorship, aimed at preventing their return, will be sabotaged and fought as Bolshevism, every beginning of self-government of the masses, as disorder, every centralized attempt to reorganize the economic system for its new tasks as 'red dictatorship in place of the brown.' " Incidentally, exactly this happened in Italy. To foresee this in 1939 shows some capacity for political understanding. Lord Vansittart, however, does not realize where our faith in ourselves really lies; not in a capacity for world domination, which we abhor, but it is faith in our ability for self-government. He ascribes quite different ideas to us, ideas that he has freely invented.

What of Vansittart's other quotations demonstrating the German feeling of superiority implicit in our anti-Nazi ideas? Maybe he has us there. In the pamphlet, following the remarks about the German revolution, we find the following: "In this *the most highly developed industrial country in the old world,* the development of the productive machine and the existing social contradictions long ago put socialism on the agenda of history." Once again Vansittart quotes only the beginning of the sentence. But in order to play his puzzle game he makes out of the reasons which we give for socialism in Germany, a demand for German world domination by juxtaposing another fragmentary quotation torn from its context. Thus we have Vansittart: "The new German hegemony is based on the old grounds that Germany is 'the most highly industrialized country in the Old World' that the historical and cultural conditions of Germany,' and the 'general educational and cultural level' of the masses entitles them to take precedence over lesser breeds—such as the Russians. (Another echo of Marx.)"

The second and third quotations are taken from the original pamphlet, but they are applied to an entirely different discussion. Both of these two phrases are to be found in a section of the second chapter of the pamphlet which discusses inner political problems in Germany, specifically, how the achievements of the revolution can be preserved. The pamphlet points out that the German revolution like every revolution in history will be forced to combat counter-revolutionary attack. There is, in this connection, a critical discussion of the experience of the Russian revolution, demonstrating how easy it is to go from a revolutionary democracy to a total party dictatorship. After warning that the revolutionaries should "not for one moment or in any sphere" surrender the democratic institutions they have just won, the authors of the pamphlet describe three safeguards that exist in Germany against a new totalitarian danger.

The first safeguard is the stage of economic development which Germany has reached which will eliminate the necessity of a long period of intense sacrifice to achieve industrialization. Second, the broader social basis for the German revolution is cited. Whereas, in 1917, in Russia the working class was a small minority, in Germany it includes the great majority of the nation. And "the third and most important safeguard lies in *the historical and cultural* background in Germany and in the resultant desire for freedom of the people and of the socialist leaders themselves. The majority of the German working classes and the German intelligentsia have, on the basis of their *general educational and cultural level* and partly also on the basis of *democratic traditions* never accepted fascist totalitarianism. After its defeat they will bitterly oppose every attempt to rob them in the name of a new totalitarianism of the freedom and self-government which they have just regained." (The pamphlet does, of course, recognize the U.S.S.R. as a potential ally in the coming war.)

Here we have crypto-pan-Germanism. An argument against any form of totalitarian rule, from the right or from the left, becomes in Vansittart's writing the claim "to take precedence over lesser breeds—such as the Russians."

The last long quotation from the pamphlet about the people of Central and Eastern Europe finds itself in the following context: "The first international task of the German revolution will be the liquidation of German imperialism." German socialists, the pamphlet continues, clearly recognize the principle of the right of self-determination of all peoples, including the right of the Hitler-annexed German districts to separate themselves from Germany. It goes on to say that German socialists must make no attempt to force economic and political cooperation upon the peoples of Central and Eastern Europe, because only thus can they hope to prevent the hatred of those people against fascism from turning also against revolutionary Germany. Experience with the Versailles organization of Europe is touched on in describing the aims of a European federation: "The democratic principle in the national question is the right of self-determination for all peoples. *But the people of Central and Eastern Europe live so inextricably mixed together that any attempt at drawing frontiers along these lines would be attended with the greatest technical difficulties, but also many of them are so small that their national states could not and cannot exist independently.*" Vansittart quotes this sentence as a crypto-pan-Germanist claim to dominate by "sheer German virtue." But the next sentence in the pamphlet continues: "The Versailles frontiers drove this contradiction into the foreground. First of all it created a whole series of economically impossible little states and thereby a series of customs barriers which economically ruined Central and Eastern Europe. Second, it not only did not draw the frontiers of these small states entirely in accord with self-determination, which would be an impossible feat, but it modified them to a great extent according to strategic, economic and other considerations favorable to the allies of the victorious powers."

The pamphlet explains how these contradictions created by the Versailles order were painstakingly utilized by the fascists with the help of German monopolists to set up a regime of brutal national oppression and the most ruthless economic exploitation of the small nations. It elaborates further: "There is an insoluble conflict between the demands of national self-determination and the demands of economic cooperation in this area only as long as the solution is sought on the level of national states. A truly democratic solution taking the right of self-determination of all nations into account simultaneously can only be federal and can only have as its goal free cooperation of the various nations with extensive self-government but with economic cooperation and without divisive customs' and military borders." It remains Vansittart's secret in what way this is "getting uncomfortably near Frederick II and 'unjustified existences.' "

Vansittart gives another example of crypto-pan-Germanism, the chapter entitled "How to Beat Hitler Politically," in my book, "Will Germany Crack?" If "The Coming World War" was "insidious expansionism," "Will Germany Crack?" is a "tendencious book." Lord Vansittart writes: "In return for the sort of program required by neo-expansionism and 'revolutionary' hegemony, he [Paul Hagen] has the temerity to tell us 'How to beat Hitler politically.' We do not need the advice, because we are going to beat Hitler militarily; and in Germany we must include all schemers for world-domination, even the left-handed ones." * And further, "The crypto-pan-Germanism of most German politically-minded refugees—most refugees are not politically-minded—and of their Anglo-Saxon and German-American partisans requires constant vigilance and unbending opposition. I speak for all the oppressed peoples of Europe when I declare that none of them will for a moment tolerate being tied to any Germany in any form after this war and they will be right. They may consider collaboration at some future and unspecified date when Germany has been thoroughly broken of all dreams and deprived of all means of leadership whether by force of arms or by rigging revolutions or markets. We and they will resist uncompromisingly any attempt to federalize Europe with Germany to suit Herr Hagen's book." †

It is not necessary to unravel this new puzzle. It unravels itself and in addition I offer this book, written long before the publication of Vansittart's revelations as evidence. The reader may check in

* *Ibid.*, page 87.
† *Ibid.*, pages 87-88.

it the accuracy of Vansittart's second item of evidence for crypto-pan-Germanism.

This is not a quarrel between two philosophies. It is useless to argue whether war is "essentially a clash between economic antagonisms." I believe, as I have pointed out in this book that wars are co-determined by other historical and moral factors and by traditions. It may be that we have had illusions about the future significance of the German revolution. In 1939, when "The Coming World War" was written we spoke of that revolution's "key position." Today it is still important, but less important than the European revolution against the Nazis which the war has prepared. This book is evidence of an effort to revise pre-war illusions. But that is not the point either.

The point is that *what Vansittart has really done has been to falsify. He has twisted the chain of thought which I and my friends developed into exactly the contrary.*

Perhaps Lord Vansittart should be given the benefit of the doubt. Eager though he may be to prove the degradation of the German character, could he consciously have played the puzzle game described? He might have been taken in by a falsification already in existence. A zealous group of Vansittartites in London, calling themselves "The Fight for Freedom Committee," in 1942 prepared a brief document composed of carefully chosen quotations from "The Coming World War," translated into English and interspersed with comment and interpretation. This document was sent to government officials in Britain and other United Nations, with the idea of discrediting the authors of the original German pamphlet. For a description of the quality of the editing of this document, I shall quote from a public statement about it made in London by the well-known Belgian Socialist, Mr. Louis de Brouckére, former president of the Labor and Socialist International. ". . . I have also reread the comment and am struck by the contradiction between text and comment, which is sometimes direct. The author of the comment has clearly 'interpreted' the sentences that shocked him, and has finally persuaded himself, as it happens if passions get excited, that what was said in his at least risky interpretation was said in the memorandum itself. We know where that method of logic leads and how much it permits one to find in the most innocent text!"* The "Fight for Freedom Committee" document has been responsible for a great deal of mischief. In peacetime, literary political falsifications are confusing and disturbing. In wartime, they are pure poison. It must have been this document which led a certain Mr. Cameron writing in the New York *Journal-American* in a cryptic piece, devoted primarily to castigation of the Office of War In-

---

* *Decency in Socialist Controversies,* by Louis de Brouckére, published by Auslandsbuero, Neu Beginnen, London N.2. 10, Devon Rise, October 14, 1942.

formation to accuse me, without mentioning my name, of wanting to oust Hitler so that I could occupy his seat.*

So, it may be that this secondary document was the source of Lord Vansittart's mistakes.

It is strange in any case for the former chief of the British Secret Service to rely on such flimsy evidence. Can we hope that Lord Vansittart, upon finding out his mistake, will correct it? We shall have to wait and see. But we can hardly expect the pattern of thought learned in this life to change any more. Thoughts are built upon fantasy; single facts do not count. Facts can be shifted around at will; if some do not fit, others will, for the emotional desire to prove a thesis is too great. On too many pages of Lord Vansittart's book the reader will find misjudgments and misstatements like those exposing the alleged crypto-pan-Germanism.

* *New York Journal-American*, May 23, 1943.